Palgrave Studies in Europe

Series Editors
Michelle Egan
American University
Washington, DC, USA

Neill Nugent
Manchester Metropolitan University
Manchester, UK

William E. Paterson
Aston University
Birmingham, UK

Following on the sustained success of the acclaimed European Union Series, which essentially publishes research-based textbooks, Palgrave Studies in European Union Politics publishes cutting edge research-driven monographs. The remit of the series is broadly defined, both in terms of subject and academic discipline. All topics of significance concerning the nature and operation of the European Union potentially fall within the scope of the series. The series is multidisciplinary to reflect the growing importance of the EU as a political, economic and social phenomenon.

More information about this series at
http://www.springer.com/series/14629

Nathalie Tocci

Framing the EU Global Strategy

A Stronger Europe in a Fragile World

Nathalie Tocci
Istituto Affari Internazionali
Rome
Italy

Palgrave Studies in European Union Politics
ISBN 978-3-319-55585-0   ISBN 978-3-319-55586-7   (eBook)
DOI 10.1007/978-3-319-55586-7

Library of Congress Control Number: 2017939549

This Palgrave Macmillan imprint is published by Springer Nature
The registered company is Springer International Publishing AG
The registered company address is: Gewerbestrasse 11, 6330 Cham, Switzerland

To Diego and Kike
Without whom none of this would have been possible

FOREWORD

Reading Nathalie's book, all the images and memories of these two years came back to me—but one above all: the incredibly intense days between the decision of the UK voters to leave the European Union and the European Council of June 28th where I presented the Global Strategy. This book testifies the unprecedented collective effort that has led to the text of the EU Global Strategy for foreign and security policy: over fifty public events in all Member States, countless rounds of consultations with governments, institutions, think tanks, experts and European citizens from all walks of life. All such work suddenly came into question after the "Brexit" vote.

I will never forget the hours after the referendum, the conversations with Nathalie and with my staff, with the presidents of the European institutions, with ministers from most Member States and with our British friends. Through those hours, we realised the decision we were taking was not simply about the European Council's agenda, it was not about procedures, nor was it about getting the best media coverage for the Strategy. We all realised there was one thing Europe could not afford after the vote, and that was uncertainty. With the British referendum, the need for a common strategy was even greater than before.

We needed—and we still need—to look beyond this self-induced crisis of European integration and to focus on what binds us together: the shared interests and the values driving our common foreign policy; our unparalleled strength, as the First-World economy, the largest global investor in humanitarian aid and development cooperation, a global security provider with a truly global diplomatic network. We need to focus on the immense untapped potential of a more joined-up European Union. We need to move from a shared vision to common action.

As Nathalie shows, throughout the process, the need for a Global Strategy became clearer and clearer to all. And six months after the presentation of the document, the twenty-eight Heads of State and Government have approved my proposals for implementing the Strategy in the field of security and defence. It is a major leap forward for European cooperation—and eventually, integration—on defence matters. The process leading to the Global Strategy has helped build consensus on a set of concrete measures and on their rationale. Instead of getting stuck into never-ending ideological debates or exhausting negotiations on revising the Treaties, we moved pretty steadily from principles to practice—to finally get things done, where it really matters.

The implementation of the Strategy is now under way in all sectors, from fostering resilience to public diplomacy, from a more joined-up development cooperation to a rethinking of global governance. The European Union of security and defence can be a major building block to relaunch the process of European integration, but it cannot be the only one. Europe can deliver on our citizens' and our partners' needs only when it acts as a true Union, at national and European levels, with our hard and soft power, in our external and internal policies alike. Europe delivers only when it is united.

In the days following the British referendum, the ultimate decision on whether to move forward with the presentation of the EUGS belonged to me—but the process leading to the decision was truly collective, just like the whole process leading to Global Strategy. We did it the European way. The process had to be inclusive, taking into account as many voices as we could. At the same time, inclusiveness had to go together with incisiveness: we had to avoid getting stuck on reciprocal vetoes, aiming for the most ambitious outcome. I believe the Strategy manages to be both inclusive and incisive. It shows a united and decisive Union, Europe at its best.

It would be impossible to recall all the people who contributed to this work. My heartfelt thanks go to Javier Solana, for his guidance, encouragement and inspiration. Nathalie holds a very special place in this story: she has my gratitude not only for the incredible work she has done but also for the energy and the patience she has put in it, for our long con-versations, her good spirits and her own "resilience". She has set up, steered and accompanied this collective process, step by step. This book tells the story of the Global Strategy from a unique and privileged per-spective. It provides the reader with a special insight into the debates and the decisions that shaped up the Strategy. In times of disillusion and dis-enchantment, it tells a different, true story about our Union: the positive story of a Union that delivers, together.

Brussels   Federica Mogherini

ACKNOWLEDGEMENTS

Many are the people I should thank, not just for this book but also for all the work that went into the story that it tells. The list would be very long, far too long, so let me limit it to those who made a tough two years of work not only possible but thoroughly enjoyable. Let me thank my closest colleagues in the EU strategic reflection process, Alfredo Conte from the Strategic Planning Division of the European External Action Service, Enrico Petrocelli from HRVP Federica Mogherini's Cabinet and Antonio Missiroli, the director of the EU Institute for Security Studies. Ours was an all-Italian team that came about more by coincidence than by design. I couldn't have been luckier to work with such a fun and committed group, each one of us with his or her added value. I would also like to thank Robert Cooper, the main author of the 2003 European Security Strategy, both for his advice on how to handle the strategic reflection and for his precious comments on this manuscript. Heartfelt thanks to the Istituto Affari Internazionali (IAI), my home base. IAI was incredibly generous with me: not only did it live with the fact that its deputy director was often at large in these years, but also my colleagues in the Institute helped me enormously behind the scenes with the content of the Strategy, each one in his or her area of expertise. The biggest thank you goes to Federica Mogherini, for the opportunity of a lifetime. The task she entrusted me with was enormous. I did my very best to live up to her expectations and trust in me. Last and most important of all, I want to thank all my family, and above all my husband Enrique and my son Diego, for their patience, love and understanding each and every day over these years. Without them, I would have never been able to seize the opportunity that Federica gave me. It is to them that this book is dedicated.

CONTENTS

CHAPTER 1

Introduction

How It All Began

I recall the first conversation with Federica Mogherini on what was to become the EU Global Strategy (EUGS) in September 2014. At the time, she was the Italian Minister of Foreign Affairs, recently designated by the European Council as High Representative of the Union for Foreign Affairs and Security Policy/Vice-President of the European Commission (HRVP). I was her advisor on strategy, juggling my time between the Italian Ministry of Foreign Affairs and my job as the Deputy Director of the Istituto Affari Internazionali (IAI) in Rome.

When I asked her whether she might be interested in embarking on a revision of the 2003 European Security Strategy (ESS), her response was immediately and unambiguously positive. In fact, she often complained about the tendency of political leaders in Europe to constantly jump from one crisis to the next. Already back then, there was no shortage of crises in and around Europe. The summer of 2014 was hot in Ukraine, Syria, Gaza and Libya, to mention a few, and European leaders were constantly flying from one capital to the next, scrambling at once to make sense of what was going on and do the best they could to extinguish the multiple fires. Those fires still burn. In most cases, they have spread. The crises of 2014 have been joined by many others, be it the self-styled "Islamic State of Iraq and Syria" (ISIS) also known by its Arabic acronym Da'esh, the war in Yemen or the relentless sequence of terror attacks in Paris, Brussels, Berlin, Tunis, Dhaka, Istanbul and Baghdad,

© The Author(s) 2017
N. Tocci, *Framing the EU Global Strategy*, Palgrave Studies
in European Union Politics, DOI 10.1007/978-3-319-55586-7_1

among others. Reacting to crises is a hard and unavoidable fact of political life. But is tactic and reaction the only way forward? To paraphrase Sun Tzu, while a strategy bereft of tactic is the slowest route to victory in foreign policy, isn't tactic without strategy just the noise before defeat? Sun Tzu's dictum clearly resonated with Federica from the very start.

I resumed the conversation with her in January 2015, when I began my work as her Special Advisor with the specific responsibility of coordinating the work on a new Strategy on foreign and security policy as well as reaching out to the broader foreign policy community, including think tanks, universities and civil society groups. Over the last two years, much of my time has been spent on what became the EU strategic reflection process, which gave birth to the EU Global Strategy, alongside my work at IAI. The Strategy was presented and welcomed by the European Council in June 2016, formally replacing its predecessor, the 2003 ESS. As I wrote this book in the fall of 2016, the EU was making its first steps on the implementation of the EUGS.

THE AIM OF THIS BOOK

Both the ESS and the EU Global Strategy have and are still receiving considerable academic and policy interest. The ESS has been the subject of a prolific academic and policy literature. Studies on the ESS have spanned political science, international relations and European studies, as well as being dissected in countless doctoral dissertations over the years. Detailed exposés include Bailes (2005), Biscop (2005), Biscop and Andersson (2008), de Vasconcelos (2009) and Biscop (2015). These and other works are "must-read" pieces for any student, scholar or practitioner wishing to understand the ESS, as well as its follow-up, the 2008 Implementation Report (HR 2003, 2008) and more broadly European foreign policy. True to tradition in European studies, a rich literature is already developing rapidly on the EU Global Strategy. The EUGS was still hot off the press when several journal special issues went to print, for instance (The International Spectator 2016; Dijkstra 2016).

This book does not aim to recount this rich literature. Instead, by taking as its reference point the ESS, this book tells the story of and behind the EUGS, tracing the troubled journey which took the EU from one major strategic document to its sequel thirteen years later. This journey is made by comparing the political context (the "why"), the strategy-making process (the "how"), the actual content (the "what") and the respective follow-ups (the "what next"), underpinning these two major EU strategic exercises and documents.

I have written this book as the outcome of a very personal experience as a scholar at the Istituto Affari Internazionali (IAI) and as Special Advisor to the High Representative of the Union for Foreign Affairs and Security Policy/Vice-President of the European Commission (HRVP). On behalf of HRVP Federica Mogherini, I coordinated the work and drafted both the 2015 EU strategic assessment (see Annex A) and the 2016 EUGS (see Annex B). It is because of this practical experience, that as a scholar, I wanted to share my thoughts with students and fellow academics and analysts. Why does an international player like the European Union produce a foreign and security policy strategy? How does it do so? What does its strategy say? And how does the EU aim to pursue it? By taking these basic questions about any strategy as its starting point, this book tells the story of the EUGS, compared to its predecessor, the ESS.

It has been 13 years since the EU produced its first foreign policy strategy—the 2003 ESS—under then High Representative (HR) Javier Solana. However, the EU Global Strategy, as the title itself suggests, is the first of its kind. It is a document drafted by a High Representative who is the Chair of the Foreign Affairs Council (including the informal Defence Council and the Development Council) *and* Vice-President of the European Commission: it is a process and a product that has brought together *both* the EU Member States and the European Commission. Whereas Javier Solana presented a European *Security* Strategy because he was "only" the EU High Representative for the Common Foreign and *Security* Policy of the Union, Federica Mogherini set out to produce a far more comprehensive EU *Global* Strategy, making full use of the multiple hats entrusted to her by the Lisbon Treaty. Generally, it is states that produce strategies. Moreover, such strategies normally focus only on security, even if broadly construed. In this case, the EU is neither a state nor an international organisation, but a hybrid mix between the two. Furthermore, the strategy that it produced was not limited to security but encompassed all dimensions of foreign policy in the broadest sense. The complexity of this exercise can only be fully grasped through an inside lens into the process.

Added to this, the strategic reflection which gave birth to the EUGS did not involve only official stakeholders. The two elements of my job description—as the coordinator of the EUGS process and responsible for outreach to think tanks—were always meant to be connected. The strategic reflection was meant to and did involve virtually all Member States including governments, ministries and parliaments, as well as the broader foreign policy community, from academia to think tanks, and from civil society to the media. The EUGS was followed closely also outside the Union, from Washington, Tokyo, Brasilia, Canberra and Moscow to places closer to home such as Ankara, Oslo, Tunis, Tbilisi, Kiev and Belgrade among others.

This book tells the inside story of this adventure, seeking to make students and scholars, practitioners and interested observers within and outside the EU aware of the politics, the process, the content and the future perspectives of the EUGS, compared to the ESS. This book includes in its annexes the two texts produced by the EU strategic reflection: the June 2015 strategic assessment and the June 2016 EUGS. It reproduces these two documents—without their respective executive summaries— for easy reference to the reader, given they are often cited in this work. As said, the aim of this book is precisely to tell the story of and behind these two documents.

But the rationale of this book does not stop here.

This is and has been a deeply enriching experience for me. Entrusting a project of this magnitude to an outside scholar was certainly not an obvious, less still an uncontested, choice by the HRVP. I distinctly remember the vocal insistence of one senior official to set up an "editorial committee" for the drafting of the Strategy. According to my interlocutor, the proposed members of such an Editorial Committee would have been, other than myself, several (male) retired diplomats. The motivation behind the suggestion was fairly obvious: How could the HRVP entrust the coordination and drafting of such a document to an outsider of the institutional machinery? I never felt any personal animosity towards myself, quite the contrary. I rather read this as an understandable, perhaps inevitable, instinct from any institutional body—in this case the European Union—to contain if not expel a foreign element. When, with the backing of the HRVP of course, I resisted the attempt of being surrounded by a group of experienced men that would control my work, I saw a look of sheer panic in the eyes of my interlocutor. All he could mutter was "but Nathalie, you cannot do this alone…what if you get ill?!"

Thankfully that did not happen. Over the last two years, I often felt like a fly, alighting here and there on the institutional ointment of Brussels, and now and then getting caught in it. I had privileged access to the European External Action Service (EEAS), the Commission, the Council and the Parliament, as well as to the politics and institutions of Member States, and interested external countries. I consulted all 28 Member States—including governments, ministries and parliaments, travelling to most capitals. The EUGS took me close to home, to Serbia, Turkey, Georgia, Norway and Israel, and further afield to the USA, Japan, Brazil and Australia, and I consulted with organisations such as the United Nations (UN), the North Atlantic Treaty Organization (NATO) and the Organization for Security and Cooperation in Europe (OSCE). I was part of a vibrant debate within the wider foreign policy community, from academia to think tanks, and from civil society to the media.

As a privileged player in this process, and yet as an outside observer of the official machinery and a scholar in "normal life", I wanted to use the lens of the EUGS, and its comparison with the ESS, to tell a broader story about the European Union's foreign policy and its functioning, both internally and vis-à-vis the outside world. My hybrid role as an insider and outsider gave me access to and knowledge of a wide range of complex structures and actors, all the while remaining sufficiently detached from official processes to retain, I hope, an external observer's eye on what surrounded me. This book reflects this hybrid nature: while written by and for students and scholars, it does not look like a classic scholarly piece of work. I rather used implicitly my academic background to recount a personal practical experience at the heart of EU foreign policy making. It is precisely in view of this hybrid nature and experience that I hope this book will make a contribution to the literature on the European Union.

All the insights gained from this intense process cannot be captured in a twenty-page document: the EU Global Strategy itself. I feel enormously privileged to have been entrusted this role by the HRVP. The very least I can do is share this experience with interested readers.

REFERENCES

Bailes, Alison J.K. 2005. *The European Security Strategy: An Evolutionary History*. SIPRI Policy Paper No. 10. Stockholm: SIPRI. http://books.sipri. org/product_info?c_product_id=190.

Biscop, Sven. 2005. *The European Security Strategy: A Global Agenda for Positive Power*. Aldershot: Ashgate.

Biscop, Sven, and Jan Joell Andersson, eds. 2008. *The EU and the European Security Strategy: Forging a Global Europe*. London: Routledge.

Biscop, Sven. 2015. *Peace Without Money, War Without Americans: Can European Strategy Cope?* London: Ashgate.

de Vasconcelos, Alvaro, ed. 2009. *The European Security Strategy 2003–2008: Building on Common Interests*. EUISS Report No. 5. Paris: EUISS.http://www.iss.europa.eu/uploads/media/ISS_Report_05.pdf.

Dijkstra, Hylke. 2016. Introduction: One-and-a-half Cheers for the EU Global Strategy. *Contemporary Security Policy* 37 (3): 369–373. doi:10.1080/13523260.2016.1244241.

EU High Representative. 2003. *A Secure Europe in a Better World. European Security Strategy*. December. https://www.consilium.europa.eu/uedocs/cmsUpload/78367.pdf.

EU High Representative. 2008. *Report on the Implementation of the European Security Strategy: Providing Security in a Changing World*, 11 December. http://www.consilium.europa.eu/uedocs/cms_data/docs/pressdata/en/reports/104630.pdf.

The International Spectator. 2016. The European Union Global Strategy. *The International Spectator* 51 (3): 1–54.

CHAPTER 2

Why Have a Strategy?

When I began to work on the EUGS, one of the first things I did was to phone up Robert Cooper. Robert, who in 2003 was the Director General for External and Politico-Military Affairs at the General Secretariat of the EU Council of Ministers, was the main drafter of HR Solana's European Security Strategy (ESS). Notwithstanding all the differences between then and now, his advice, probably more than anyone else's, was precious to me. Indeed, the conversation was an eye-opener.

The very first thing he asked me was: "why are you doing this?". The question had not been raised openly in conversation with HRVP Mogherini until then. But of course, the political rationale for undertaking a Strategy had been implicit in our discussions, and the first steps she made in the endeavour. As Robert rightly pointed out, clarity in the political purpose of an exercise such as this was of fundamental importance. Such political purpose would not be stated, black-on-white, in the Strategy itself. But it would inform both the design of the process and ultimately the content of the document itself. And the political rationale for a strategy is intimately connected to the geopolitical context in which it is embedded. Any strategy, while being a long-term vision, is the daughter of its time.

© The Author(s) 2017   7
N. Tocci, *Framing the EU Global Strategy*, Palgrave Studies in European Union Politics, DOI 10.1007/978-3-319-55586-7_2

THE POLITICAL RATIONALE FOR THE EUROPEAN SECURITY STRATEGY

The ESS was born in 2003, at a specific historical moment. The European Union was at its height. The euro had started circulating the previous year, marking the most ambitious step of the integration project since the 1957 Treaty of Rome (Tsoukalis 2016: 30–32). At the same time, the Union was on the eve of enlargement to the countries of Central and Eastern Europe. The success of that process, 1 year later, would mark the long-sought reunification of Europe after half a century of Cold War divide. The euro and the eastern enlargement demonstrated tangibly the depth and breadth of the European project. Enlargement gave a new lease of life to the European narrative of peace and security on the continent, at a time in which the political salience of the traditional peace narrative—Franco-German reconciliation—was losing power as its success over the decades caused it to be taken for granted. The success of the euro in its first years corroborated a second narrative, that of European prosperity through integration. Not only was the single currency the most palpable proof of European integration, but it was also accompanied by years of sustained economic growth during most of the 2000s. The concurrency of the euro and the eastern enlargement also invalidated the thesis that the widening and deepening of the EU were mutually incompatible. Both could be pursued at the same time for the benefit of all. True, already back then some complained about the unwieldy Brussels bureaucracy and the Union's democratic deficit. But the EU's legitimacy largely rested on its output (Schmidt 2013). No surprise that the opening line of the ESS read: "Europe has never been so prosperous, so secure, nor so free" (EUHR 2003: 1). That first sentence captured fully the mood of those times.

Those years were not without difficulties. The terrorist attacks of 9/11 in New York and Washington, D.C. opened the way to the most extreme period of US unilateralism to date. The writing was on the wall by the fall of 2002. The US National Security Strategy released by President George W. Bush in September that year put it bluntly: "America is fighting a war against terrorists of global reach", arguing that Washington would "act alone, if necessary" as well as "pre-emptively" (The White House 2002). Such pre-emptive and unilateral action was dramatically on display 6 months later, when in March 2003 a US-led coalition of the willing attacked Saddam Hussein's Iraq without a UN Security Council (UNSC) resolution mandating the "pre-emptive" military intervention. The Iraq War and what came with it—the violation of international law, and the invasion of a country based on false evidence, i.e. the alleged possession of weapons of mass destruction—propelled the USA to the height of its unilateral moment.

Such unilateralism left Europeans with a Shakespearean choice: to be or not to be with the USA? For some EU Member States (and most soon-to-be members from Central and Eastern Europe), sticking with Washington, no matter what, weighed more heavily than anything else. Tony Blair's UK first and foremost, alongside Silvio Berlusconi's Italy, José Maria Aznar's Spain and José Manuel Barroso's Portugal, stood out among EU-15 in favour of a US-first approach. Jacques Chirac's France and Gerhard Schröder's Germany led the widespread opposition to the violation of multilateralism and international law embodied by the US's onslaught on Iraq. The split within the Union over the Iraq War and the divisions across the Atlantic were deeply felt. Intra-European differences were painfully on show in multilateral fora, beginning with the UNSC. This triggered a deep European soul-searching about how to deal with critical security threats, such as international terrorism, while sticking to multilateralism and international law, which constitute the very moral and ideational bedrock of the European project.

HR Solana's ESS sought to pick up the pieces and rebuild intra-European and transatlantic consensus. The goal of "effective multilateralism" heralded in the ESS sought to bridge over those differences in typical European fashion. The catchphrase squared the circle of European divisions, reflecting the Franco-German insistence on multilateralism and international law, alongside the British—and American—caveat that such multilateralism had to be effective to be of any value. In sum, the 2003 ESS was the product of its times. It was imbued with the optimism of those years, while seeking a common narrative to heal the transatlantic and intra-European rift over the war in Iraq. In 2003, the geopolitical context had given rise to a clear, simple and crucially important political rationale to embark upon a ESS—rekindling European unity through a quintessentially European narrative. HR Solana saw clearly this rationale and promptly acted upon it.

The same cannot be said of the 2008 Implementation Report on the ESS. In 2008, the context was very different and did not generate a clear and compelling reason to engage in a new strategy. By late 2007, what by then had become 27 EU Member States invited HR

Solana to assess the state of play of the ESS. The aim was that of review-ing the implementation of the Strategy, notably in view of the European Security and Defence Policy (ESDP) missions and operations deployed over those 4 years. The intention of the two main proponents of this initiative—then Swedish Foreign Minister Carl Bildt and newly elected French President Nicolas Sarkozy—went much further however. Rather than simply reviewing the state of play of the ESS, France, in particular, which was gearing up to its presidency of the Council in the second half of 2008 had ambitious plans to launch a brand new ESS. But the mood in Paris was not shared elsewhere. Specifically, there was little enthusiasm for the endeavour in London and Berlin. Javier Solana himself was not keen to embark on a new ESS. Therefore, the result was a rather bland mandate by the European Council to simply review the implementation of the ESS. The context was not propitious for a new Strategy.

The change in the context during the drafting of the Implementation Report muddied the waters further, hollowing out even more the politi-cal rationale for a new Strategy. It would be incorrect to say that 2008 was devoid of foreign policy dramas: Kosovo's declaration of independ-ence, NATO's Bucharest summit and the Russo-Georgian War that fol-lowed it made it an eventful year. But rather than raising the interest in and galvanising consensus around the need for a new strategy, these events simply served to exacerbate divisions between the 27 EU Member States. Indeed, the 2008 Implementation Report was not formally endorsed by the Council, not least because Cyprus—as a non-NATO Member with traditionally close ties to Russia—objected to the wording on NATO in the text.

But the most important reason why the wind was taken out of the sails of a new ESS in 2008 was because of the global financial earthquake triggered by the collapse of Lehman Brothers in New York in September that year. Indeed, the outbreak of the global financial crisis and the ensu-ing spillover into the Eurozone by 2009–2010 distracted all high-level political attention away from foreign and security policy. The EU was entering a protracted and profound period of introspection, aimed at saving the single currency. With the Eurozone, and the European Union itself, on the line, the political space and rationale for engaging in a new Security Strategy was close to nil, both in 2008 and in the dramatic years that followed. Far from strategising, the European Council frantically jumped from one emergency meeting to the next to save the ailing euro, and with it, the European Union as a whole.

A compelling geostrategic context and a clear political awareness of it are the necessary conditions for a productive strategic reflection process. This was probably the most important lesson I drew from the ESS, compared to its 2008 sequel. In the case of 2003, the political logic was crystal clear: HR Solana embarked upon the ESS for a single and simple political reason: bridging the scarring divide created by the US-led invasion and occupation of Iraq both within the EU and across the Atlantic. The process and the content of the ESS reflected that political purpose. Indeed, the ESS contributed in no small measure to fulfilling its primary political task and mending the divide that had paralysed the Union that year. In 2008, the context was far murkier, and in the months and years that followed, the limited space for foreign policy thinking was eaten up by internal economic governance issues generated by the Eurozone crisis. As opposed to 2003, in 2008 the European Union was not ready for a new strategy.

THE POLITICAL RATIONALE FOR THE EU GLOBAL STRATEGY

Fast-forward to 2015, why did HRVP Federica Mogherini embark upon a process of strategic reflection and then produced an EU Global Strategy? By late 2014, the context was radically different once again. While the EU's internal ills were far from over, they were matched and in many ways surpassed by a dramatically deteriorating geostrategic environment. At the very least, such context meant that the opening line of the 2003 ESS—"Europe has never been so prosperous, so secure, nor so free" (EUHR 2003: 1)—was no longer true. Just like in 2003, and unlike 2008, it was the geostrategic context which generated the political need for a new strategy and crystallised the consensus for it among what by then were 28 Member States. Just like in 2003 when HR Solana understood that context and responded to it, so did HRVP Mogherini in 2015–2016. As we began working on the EU strategic reflection in 2015, retracing the thought process and political logic of 2003 was crucial in designing the process, the content and the follow-up of the EUGS. Unlike in 2003 when there was one fundamental reason to produce the ESS, in 2015–2016, there were three main reasons to produce the EUGS: to promote policy direction, to strengthen political unity and to boost the effectiveness of external actions.

POLICY DIRECTION: PROVIDING A CHART TO NAVIGATE TROUBLED WATERS

The history of the European integration project has never been smooth, with lots of major challenges having been faced over the decades. At times, these were related to the process of European integration itself. This was true in the mid-1960s, with the "empty chair crisis" in which French President Charles de Gaulle boycotted European institutions in view of France's opposition to the supranationalist turn of the European Commission. Likewise, in the 1970s German economist Herbert Giersch coined the term "Eurosclerosis" to describe the protracted economic stagnation affecting western Europe.

At other times, difficulties were driven by external developments and the EU's reaction, or rather inaction, to them. The most well-known example was in 1991, when the escalating civil war in the Balkans led the then Luxembourg Prime Minister Jacques Poos to pompously announce the "hour of Europe", only to be followed by the Community's total inability to stop the carnage, lacking as it did the institutional machinery both to develop a common analysis of the problem and to pursue a common response to it. Europeans collectively failed to act, embarrassingly leaving the job to the Anglo-French artillery under UN command and to NATO, followed by the US-brokered 1993 Dayton accords that put an end to the war in Bosnia. It came as no surprise that Europe's shame in the Balkans galvanised the 12 members of the Community at the time to establish through the 1993 Maastricht Treaty the three-pillar structure of the Union, which lasted until the 2009 Lisbon Treaty. With Maastricht, what had been a loose process of European Political Cooperation on foreign policy between Community members was upgraded into the Common Foreign and Security Policy, the second pillar of the Union. CSFP thus came to stand alongside the first Community pillar, largely centred on the single market, and the third pillar focusing on justice and home affairs.

In short, European integration has been marked and at times spurred by challenges and crises both within and beyond Europe. But never more than today has there been such a concurrence of multiple threats and challenges, within and without, whose sheer number and depth are questioning the very existence of the European project.

In late 2014, when my first conversations with Federica Mogherini on what was to become the EU Global Strategy took place, the European

Union had already been going through critical years. In 2005, France and the Netherlands voted down the EU Constitutional Treaty: the product of the Convention on the Future of Europe. The internal crisis this generated was not resolved until 2009, when the Lisbon Treaty—a marginally reworded version of the Constitutional Treaty, sanitised of the latter's most symbolic elements—entered into force. The constitutional crisis, alongside the "big bang" enlargement to Central and Eastern Europe in 2004, took its toll on the appetite for further enlargements. Romania and Bulgaria completed the eastern enlargement in 2007, and Croatia managed to enter the Union in 2013. But most other countries, both within the enlargement process and in the remit of the ENP, began suffering from the EU's "enlargement fatigue" as it became known in those years (Devrim and Schulz 2009).

Worse still, no sooner was the EU's constitutional crisis over, than the Eurozone crisis kicked in. Triggered by the 2008 global financial crisis, with Greece's revelations of its gaping public finance holes, by 2009 markets began speculating on the viability of the Eurozone (Tsoukalis 2016). Beyond the specific vulnerabilities of the EU Member States at the geographical periphery of the Union, notably Portugal, Ireland, Greece and Spain, as well as Italy and shortly afterwards followed by Cyprus, the crisis raised a deeper question about the viability of a European monetary union. The Eurozone crisis exposed the fatal flaws of a monetary union between widely different economies joined by a single currency without, however, a unified fiscal policy to compensate for these variations. The very existence of the EU's most visible achievement, half-baked as it was—the Euro—was at stake. If the Euro fell, it risked bringing down with it the entire European edifice.

If this were not enough, the EU's neighbourhood, both to the east and to the south, plunged into unprecedented chaos and violence. To the east, as the EU approached the completion of its association process with the Eastern Partnership countries, notably Ukraine, the illusion of partnership between the EU and Russia dissolved (see Annex A: 107 and 115). That Russia had never accepted the notion of NATO's expansion to the east was well known. Indeed, the 2008 Bucharest Summit, in which NATO declared that Georgia and Ukraine "will become" allies one day, triggered visible displeasure in Moscow. NATO was and will remain viewed with deep suspicion and animosity by Russians. But by then, EU enlargement began generating similar misgivings in Moscow. Associated as it was with democratisation, the EU started being viewed with suspicion in Moscow, which saw in its policies a cause of "colour revolutions" which could have eventually spilled into Russia proper, provoking regime change there too. The sequence of events is well known. As Kiev was on the verge of signing its Deep and Comprehensive Free Trade Agreement with the EU in the fall of 2013, Russian President Vladimir Putin put forward to his Ukrainian counterpart "an offer he couldn't refuse". The promise of $15bn in aid and a one-third reduction in Russian gas prices brought Ukrainian President Viktor Yanukovych joyfully to his knees. Ukraine's backtracking from the EU triggered escalating popular protests in Kiev's Maidan square, which ultimately led to the collapse of Yanukovych's government in February 2014. This was followed by Russia's annexation of Crimea in March and its intervention in eastern Ukraine since then.

The south of the Union fared no better (see Annex A: 107 and 116–117). By late 2011, hopes for an Arab spring had started evaporating, opening the way to diametrically different seasonal or historical analogies being used instead. By the summer of 2011, Syria spiralled into an all-out civil war, which saw an accelerating outflow of internally displaced persons within Syria, and of Syrian refugees in Turkey, Lebanon and Jordan. Two years later, Egypt succumbed to a full-blown military coup which ousted the elected—albeit admittedly incompetent—President Mohammed Morsi and established an even harsher authoritarian regime than the one which existed before the 2011 uprising. After its parliamentary elections in early 2014, Libya, which had been largely abandoned by Europeans and Americans after NATO's intervention and the ouster of Muammar Ghaddafi in 2011, gradually descended into civil war. In 2014, Israel waged war, again, on Gaza; Saudi Arabia attacked Yemen's Houthis, and more broadly the regional rivalry between Saudi Arabia and Iran escalated, with Syrians, Yemenis and plummeting oil revenues being the most obvious casualties. Also in 2014, the ruptures within al-Qaeda in the Levant coupled with the spread of sectarianism and ungoverned spaces in Iraq and Syria led to the establishment of ISIS, later self-renamed Islamic State. While Tunisia was left standing as the only shimmer of light in a darkening region, far from an Arab spring, all the talk began revolving around an Arab winter or a Middle Eastern version of Europe's 30 years' war.

As the Middle East imploded, the European Union, a few kilometres away from its shores, was not immune. Beginning with the Charlie Hebdo massacre in January 2015, to be followed by a gruesome sequence of terrorist attacks in Paris, Brussels, Nice and elsewhere, the implosion of the Middle East began reverberating into Europe too. This was not so much the case of Islamic State terrorists travelling from Mosul or Raqqa to carry out their bloody attacks in Europe. The problem was rather that of a growing pool of European citizens, who from being "only" depressed, marginalised or petty criminals, rapidly transformed into dangerous terrorists, intoxicated by the idea of a violent jihad, which knows no borders between the Middle East, Europe and beyond. At least since 2010, the most acute crises facing the Union have been within and at the borders of the EU itself. But the list of threats and challenges the EU is called upon to respond does not stop here.

In Asia, security tensions have been mounting (see Annex A: 108 and 119). Coming on top of a nuclear capable and unpredictable North Korea, Asian insecurity has been rising due to the changing balance of power caused by China's rise. China's economic growth is, perhaps inevitably, coming alongside greater Chinese political and military assertiveness in its own neighbourhood. This is generating a nascent competition between the USA and China in the Pacific, growing apprehension of Asian powers such as Japan, South Korea and Australia, as well as of smaller South East Asian countries such as the Philippines. The military build-up in the East and South China Seas is the most tangible manifestation of this fact. In many respects, Europe is far removed from Asia's security woes. Particularly when it comes to the US–China competition, some may think that Europe does not have a dog in the fight. Yet the EU does have a huge stake in Asian security. Europe is Asia's first economic partner, and vice versa. European prosperity thus hinges on Asian security, and therefore the Union cannot remain idle watching insecurity mount in the region.

Likewise, development and security in Africa are of paramount importance to the Union (see Annex A: 117). Africa lies at Europe's doorstep, being separated by a tiny strip of sea, which is the Mediterranean. While Africa is and should be viewed as a land of opportunity for Africans and for the wider world, there remain plenty of problems in the continent, which the Union must grapple with. In many regions, African economic development lags behind the continent's demographic growth. The persistence of old conflicts, the emergence of new security problems connected with the spread of terrorist movements such as Boko Haram and the challenges of climate change and food insecurity all represent vital challenges and threats to Africa and to Europe alike.

Finally, the Union and its Member States must deal with wider global threats and challenges. Global financial turmoil, the outbreak of the Ebola pandemic, mounting cases of cybercrime, unspeakable humanitarian crises, natural disasters, climate change, plummeting global energy markets, persisting organised crime and the pending problems of unreformed global governance institutions, beginning with the United Nations and the International Financial Institutions, are but a few examples of our more connected, contested and complex world (see Annex A: 104–115).

The EU and its Member State cannot but react to this long list of threats and challenges. But whereas agreeing on how to react is the bread and butter of most discussions of the Foreign Affairs Council, alone it is woefully insufficient. Paradoxically, the more time is spent reacting due to the sheer number and depth of crises at hand, the more urgently its leaders feel the need for a clear direction and a proactive policy.

As mentioned in the Introduction, this need was strongly felt by the HRVP herself. From her days as the Italian Minister of Foreign Affairs, she lamented the constant and erratic mode of foreign policy reaction. She felt that European leaders and policy-makers were simply jumping from one crisis to the next, hopelessly seeking to put out one fire, only to discover the next had already broken out. In this hectic dance, the time and space to look beyond the present and address root causes and tomorrow's challenges were simply absent. It felt like being a captain of a ship in stormy waters without a chart indicating the way.

Hence, the first policy aim of the strategic reflection was that of creating the time and space to look ahead. The Strategy aimed to be the chart that the HRVP felt European foreign policy lacked and needed. Neither she nor any leader was under the illusion that a EUGS would provide a literal blueprint for action on the way ahead. A strategy is not an action plan on what to do today or tomorrow. Reaction will continue to occupy centre stage in European foreign policy and indeed international relations. But a strategy indicates the EU's broad goals and addresses the necessary means to achieve these. Equipping the EU for the future does not necessarily require the ability to predict precisely the crises of tomorrow. In fact, investing in making the EU's policies and instruments more credible, more joined-up and more responsive—as the EUGS concludes—is necessary precisely because of the unpredictability lying ahead (see Annex B: 155–161).

POLITICAL UNITY: BRIDGING OVER MULTIPLE DIVIDES

Like in 2003, today the EU is divided. This time there is not one sin-gle cleavage—as over the 2003 war in Iraq—but rather multiple ones. In view of these multiple divisions within and between the Member States, which taken together have triggered the deepest existential crisis of the European project since its inception, the EUGS sought to re-instil politi-cal unity among Europeans. If, through the strategic reflection and the EUGS, Europeans could understand one another better and agree on a shared narrative concerning the EU's role in the world, this would serve to rekindle a degree of political unity in the Union as a whole. As social constructivists would say, discourse, including strategy-making, is an identity-building exercise.

The multiple crises discussed above generated different cleavages between the Member States. The Eurozone crisis and the economic cri-sis that followed sowed unprecedented divisions and mistrust particularly between the northern and southern Member States. The exposure of the wide economic divergences between Eurozone members, and the fiscal laxity displayed, and in the case of Greece concealed, by some Member States, generated huge distrust in the north, notably in Germany, towards southern members. The result was the imposition of top-down harsh austerity measures through a series of packs, and pacts shoved down the throats of southern economies on the brink. In particular, the activation of the Troika—the Commission, the European Central Bank and the International Monetary Fund—in Greece, Cyprus, Portugal, Spain and Ireland, and the intergovernmental Fiscal Compact aimed at enshrin-ing fiscal rigour in the constitutions of Eurozone members were despised measures by many members at the geographical periphery of the Union. These steps contributed in no small measure in triggering the deepest economic crisis since the 1930s in these countries, generating an unprec-edented wave of antipathy towards the north, and Germany in particu-lar. The result was a dialogue of the deaf. Germany spoke the ordo-liberal language of austerity and adamantly resisted moves towards a "transfer union" in which richer and more responsible "creditors" had to bail out the irresponsible fiscal laxity of the "debtors" (Schmidt 2016). Southern European countries finger pointed Germany's gains reaped from the com-petitive advantage of being part of a monetary union with weaker econ-omies and advocated growth for all through an end of austerity. They supported the completion of the Eurozone project through a banking union, a fiscal union and a political union, as advocated by the four presidents of the Union in 2012 (Van Rompuy et al. 2012).

Beyond putting out the immediate fire that risked bringing down the Eurozone by enshrining fiscal consolidation and making the first steps towards a banking union, the divide between the Member States persists. There has been no sign of abating of the north–south divide over austerity versus growth. The deep cleavage over the conduct of economic policy within the Union has been reflected in a standstill over the Euro area's governance. The banking union is only partially complete, while precious little has been done to move towards a fiscal or a political union as had been championed by the four former presidents of EU institutions in 2012, and later revised into the five presidents report in 2015 (Van Rompuy et al. 2012; Juncker et al. 2015). In other words, having done the bare minimum to avoid falling into the abyss, the deep cleavage between the Member States over how to handle the economy has left the Union dangerously tinkering at its edges.

The quagmire to the east sowed further divisions. The crisis over Ukraine exposed old divisions within the EU, notably between the southern/western and northern/eastern Member States. Russia has always been viewed with suspicion in most central, eastern and northern European countries. Historical memories are understandably entrenched. They violently resurfaced with the events in Ukraine and more broadly by an assertive Russia that seemed to have suddenly re-awoken from its post-Cold War torpor. These fears were lost on the other Member States in the south and west of the Union. For these countries, Russia was a serious commercial partner and an indispensable energy provider. This meant that Russia was certainly not viewed as a threat, if anything as a partner. Still in the fall of 2014, after the annexation of Crimea and the outbreak of violence in Donbass, many Europeans, notably from southern and western Europe, insisted on referring to Russia as a "strategic partner", sending shockwaves in the Baltics, Poland, Sweden and others. Furthermore, southern European relations with eastern Europe had never been particularly strong. This meant that, while never openly stated, the sovereignty of countries such as Ukraine, Moldova or Georgia was hardly viewed as a strategic priority by the southern Member States. Deep down, many in these countries believe that Russia has a rightful claim to its "zone of influence" in eastern Europe. In other words, a heightened threat perception in the east, coupled with a lack of empathy in the south towards the east's predicament, generated another scarring divide in the EU between those Member States feeling the heat of Russia's assertiveness in the east and those wishing to reset the clock back to pre-2014 normality, i.e. before Russia's annexation of Crimea. Had the EUGS been written in 2014, I am sure this would have been by far the most divisive issue.

The imploding North Africa and the Middle East, and the "refugee crisis" this generated, brought about a third cleavage, this time between the east and the west. Since its first entry into force in 1997, the Dublin regulation, subsequently revised in 2003 and 2013, foresees that refugees seeking international protection in the EU can only apply for asylum in the first country of arrival in the Union. Up until the early 2010s, the system had its logic. On the one hand, the northern Member States such as Germany, Sweden and the Netherlands hosted far greater number of migrants than the southern Member States. Therefore, it was only fair to begin redressing the imbalance by calling upon the southern Member States to absorb new arrivals. Furthermore, throughout the 1990s and 2000s, migrants did not only or even predominantly come from North Africa, sub-Saharan Africa and the Middle East, but also from the Balkans, Afghanistan and Asia. In other words, not all made their way into the EU across the Mediterranean to Europe's southern shores, but arrived through multiple entry points into the Union. On the other hand, southern European economies such as Greece and Spain had witnessed high growth rates in the 1990s and 2000s, thus being able to absorb the relatively contained numbers of migrants that arrived to their shores in those years.

The Eurozone crisis coupled with the imploding Middle East broke the logic that had underpinned the Dublin system (Henry and Pastore 2014). Southern European economies, badly hit by the economic crisis, were in no position to absorb large numbers of migrants. At the same time, violence, repression and ungoverned spaces in North Africa and the Middle East led to an outpour of refugees seeking protection in Europe. Unable to reach Europe through legal channels, the only means available to them were irregular ones, crossing dangerous land and sea borders to reach the southern members of the Union, in particular, Italy and Greece. The latter began vociferously calling for European solidarity as the migrants seeking to cross into the EU rose. Greater solidarity is essential to the southern Member States on the receiving end of hundreds of thousands of migrants who seek protection in Europe, having risked their lives—often not surviving—crossing the Sahara Desert and the Mediterranean Sea. Translated into policy practice, this meant a call to set aside the Dublin regulation, which foreseeing that refugees must apply for asylum in the first EU country of arrival, practically meant that their applications had to be processed and eventually accepted solely in Greece and Italy.

German Chancellor Angela Merkel, out of need perhaps more than heart, eventually heard the call, working hand-in-glove with the European Commission to gradually move away from the Dublin system towards a system of quotas, in which the refugees entering the EU through the southern shores would be relocated to the other Member States according to their relative size and absorption capacity. The push was on the establishment of a refugee relocation mechanism within the Union, proposed first through the Commission's Agenda on Migration in 2015 and then advanced by successive European Council decisions in 2015 and 2016.

But this push sent shock waves across central and eastern Europe, and was viewed as a slap in the face by nationalist governments particularly in Hungary and Poland, and to a lesser extent Slovakia and the Czech Republic. The near absence of migration in these countries, the construction imaginary enemies to defeat, memories of top-down Soviet decisions and the presence of self-declared illiberal governments in power claiming that their erection of fences was the ultimate defence of Christian Europe from the barbarian "others" was an explosive mix. They strongly opposed all Commission plans on resettlement and relocation, more still the longer term intention to move towards a genuinely common asylum system. With Hungary upping the ante by calling a referendum on the relocation mechanism (which failed to achieve a quorum in October 2016), and Merkel losing steam after the German political backlash against her summer 2015 open door policy to refugees, the standstill over internal migration and asylum policy within the EU deepened. Italy and Greece, left alone to face the migration challenge, became increasingly resentful of the EU's lack of solidarity, feeding further Euroscepticism in the south.

In other words, to the north–south divide over the economy and the east–south/west divide over Russia, an east–west divide on the underlying values of the European project was exposed in full force by the "refugee crisis". The EU's "refugee crisis" is not a crisis of numbers. A couple of million arrivals in a Union of 500 million people may be a challenge of absorption, integration and naturalisation, but in no way does it constitute a "crisis". Saying so is deeply insulting particularly to those countries in the region that shoulder incommensurately higher burdens in incommensurately worse circumstances. If Lebanon, a fragile country of 4 million hosting over 1.5 million Syrian refugees is not in "crisis", how can a prosperous Union of 500 million define itself so due to the arrival of a few million desperate souls reaching its shores? The EU's "refugee crisis" has been a different sort of crisis. I strongly believe it is first and foremost a crisis of values, of which Europeans should feel ashamed. It is also an intra-EU crisis that has seen deep divergences emerge between the Member States, as well as the European Commission, which have prevented meaningful EU steps forward on establishing genuinely common asylum and migration policies. In other words, all the Member States agree on the need to control migration flows into the EU through border management and external migration policy. However, there has been a sharp divide between those that want to move forward on a genuine common asylum and migration system, and those who simply focus on the control of external borders aimed at stemming the inflow into the Union altogether.

Intra-EU divisions have not only emerged between the Member States, but also within them, as openly acknowledged in the 2015 strategic assessment (see Annex A: 110). Populism and Euroscepticism are not new in Europe. However, they have acquired a higher profile with the turn of the century through a potent mix of anti-immigration sentiment, post-9/11 Islamophobia, EU enlargement fatigue and the Eurozone crisis, all cast against the broader backlash against globalisation to which also non-Europeans, notably North Americans, are not immune, as evidenced by Donald Trump's 2016 presidential victory in the USA. For the first time, populist and anti-systemic Euroscepticism—or more accurately Europhobia—is becoming a mass phenomenon in several EU Member States. These anti-systemic movements do not simply position themselves "against the elites" and "with the people", but do so by challenging the very foundations of the political system, including the basic principles of representative democracy.

The tones and shades of these movements and parties differ. In southern European countries, notably Greece, Italy and Spain, they have tended to be left-leaning. Such movements are not always or necessarily anti-European. However, they have tended to blame the EU and its policy of austerity for crumbling welfare systems, soaring unemployment, precarious working conditions and anaemic or negative growth.

This has led to them to question the very legitimacy of the EU project, thus acquiring a distinct Eurosceptic spin. The rise of these parties and movements has reflected the escalation of public distrust of the EU in weak southern Eurozone economies, in which the transfer of sovereignty out of the hands of national politicians has been starkest. Data from a 2016 Pew survey are striking. Traditionally, Europhile countries such as Italy, Greece, Spain and Portugal now display the highest levels of Euroscepticism in the EU (Pew Research Center 2016). In response, and as a means of acquiring standing among their publics, emerging political entrepreneurs as well as mainstream centre-right and centre-left wing parties in the south increasingly rely on the politics of symbolism and populism. Opportunistically, the European Union has become their favourite punching ball to galvanise consent among the public.

Further north, in France, Germany, Austria or the Netherlands, far-right racist parties, from being marginal and marginalised, have risen at an astounding pace, mounting a formidable challenge to the mainstream. In this case, Euroscepticism is driven by the nationalist/sovereigntist DNA of these parties, alongside their view of the EU as a liberal force spurring the free movement of people—aka migration—as well as free trade. Governing centre-right or centre-left parties in these countries, fearful of being outflanked from the right, have tended to adopt partially populist right-wing agendas, notably with respect to migration, asylum, Islam and a resistance to free trade. In other words, even if not in government, the rise of the populist and Eurosceptic right in many northern European countries has already polluted the political and policy agenda of the mainstream.

In some central and eastern European countries, notably Hungary and Poland, nationalist, populist and Eurosceptic parties actually won elections and are in office, challenging the democratic foundations of these states and the underlying values of the EU as a whole. The EU's powerlessness vis-à-vis these developments debilitates the Union's standing and is gleefully watched by other populist authoritarian leaders outside the EU, first and foremost Russian President Vladimir Putin.

Finally, and most dramatically: Brexit. The UK's referendum campaign on EU membership and the ultimate victory of the Leave campaign signalled at once a fundamental crisis in one of the oldest European representative democracies, a dramatic political, generational and geographical split within an EU Member State, the legitimisation of the basest of nativist instincts, the opportunistic, leveraging of the politics of fear, and the weakening of the European project as a whole.

Amidst all these divisions between and within the Member States, the strategic reflection and the EUGS hoped to provide an opportunity to regenerate a degree of unity—without which there is no policy. The deep divisions between north and south, east and west, and within every EU Member State would not disappear with the EUGS of course. Nor would the strategic reflection have determined the fate of the UK referendum, although then Prime Minister David Cameron arguably could have made more of the strategic case for the UK to remain in the EU.[1] But with all its limits, the EUGS aimed to make a political contribution to the European project in times of unprecedented division. As explained in Chap. 3, this was ultimately the reason why the HRVP decided to proceed with the publication of the EUGS 48 hours after the fateful UK referendum. The Strategy both highlighted the need for unity among Europeans, but also, in and of itself, implicitly told a story of how unity is still possible. Ultimately without political unity, it would have been impossible to produce a document that brought together 28 Member States, all EU institutions and key segments of the European foreign policy community writ large.

THE BUREAUCRATIC RATIONALE: A JOINED-UP UNION

The Strategy sought to foster a more joined-up Union in external action. In 2003, the world was a fairly benign place. Europe certainly was. Hence, the 2003 ESS did not have to preoccupy itself too much with action. The action the EU was pursuing was, broadly speaking, heading in the right direction, or so it seemed at the time. While policy-makers in the early 2000s were already conscious of the failure over Iraq, the shadow of failure in the Balkans meant that quite a lot of action was already underway. Therefore, it was sufficient for the ESS to provide a shared vision that helped foster a newfound sense of political unity notably between the three largest EU Member States: France, Germany and the UK, and across the Atlantic.

In 2015–2016, the multiple crises in Europe and beyond and the multiple divisions between and within the Member States which had been caused, exacerbated or exposed by these crises meant that changing the course of action was essential. Business as usual in EU foreign policy-making could not be an option. But to change action and to deliver better results in EU foreign policy, a wide set of institutional actors had to be brought to work together far more systematically. This is the most important and interesting interpretation of what the EU "Global" Strategy meant. A Global Strategy would have to be a "whole of EU" endeavour, engaging the multiple players in their respective institutions and policy areas, within EU institutions and the Member States, which can deliver better policy results only by working more together.

This was the spirit of the Lisbon Treaty, which created the European External Action Service to act as an interface between the Member States and the European Commission and, as a blend between the two, become the nascent diplomatic service of the Union. The aim of a more joined-up Union was also behind the Lisbon Treaty's creation of a triple-hatted HR/VP, who would at once be the Vice President of the Commission, High Representative of the Union for Foreign Affairs and Security Policy and Chair of the Foreign Affairs Council, as well as the head of the European Defence Agency.

In between the drafting of what eventually became the Lisbon Treaty and its execution, there was a gap of 6 years: many seemed to have forgotten the spirit of the Convention on the Future of Europe and why many of those decisions were actually taken. The rationale behind the Lisbon Treaty needed to be reminded and the strategic reflection sought to do just that. A third aim of the exercise was, therefore, that of strengthening the Lisbon Treaty's provisions that called upon all external policy players to be brought closer together with a view to delivering more effective policy. Simply put, the Global Strategy was an attempt to implement the letter and spirit of the Lisbon Treaty in the area of foreign and security policy, hence, the emphasis on a joined-up Union both in the strategic assessment as well as in the Strategy proper (see Annex A: 127–129; Annex B: 159–161). This was a task which, according to many, the first HRVP Catherine Ashton had failed to achieve. In 2009, it was a daunting challenge. Setting up the EEAS against the Commission's brick wall, while concurrently wearing all hats designed by the Lisbon Treaty and confronting the post 2011 Arab uprisings, was no simple feat. Ashton thus focused her attention on the establishment of the EEAS as well as on her role as HR, essentially dropping almost entirely her hat as the Vice President of the European Commission, with some notable exceptions.[2] It is not the aim here to pass judgement on the choices made and steps taken by HRVP Ashton. To be fair, the Commission made her life very difficult, by jealously guarding its external action competences and resisting these to be blended with the CFSP as part of a coherent EU foreign policy. Confronted with an unproductive institutional tug of war, Ashton yielded, understandably wanting to get on with the job and do something. It is beside the point whether HRVP Ashton could have done more or better to wear fully the many hats granted to her by the Lisbon Treaty. Responsibilities for this sorry state of affairs aside, her mandate was associated with scarring divides and institutional turf wars in the Brussels beltway between the Commission and the Council, with the fledgling EEAS lacking substantive powers to effectively bring them together (Balfour 2014).

Following the 2014 European Parliament elections and the nomination of the new Commission, many were eager to turn the page. This is not to say that institutional turf wars are over, far from it. Political, institutional and personal battles are still fought, often through the use and abuse of bureaucratic procedures. But by the autumn of 2014, there was a general sense in the Brussels bubble that the moment had come for a partial timeout. The truth was that no one could succeed in achieving policy and often political aims by operating myopically in his or her silo either by elbowing others out or by simply ignoring their existence. The result of siloed approaches was sub-optimal policy outcomes for all. Particularly within the Commission, many were aware of the need for a more strategic approach to the use of the use of the potentially extremely powerful instruments at their disposal. In its absence, the result was a mix of bureaucratic inertia coupled with the uncoordinated pursuit of the political agendas of individual Commissioners. In the sorry state, the Union is in business as usual was a luxury they could not afford.

The strategic reflection leading to the EUGS sought to translate this theoretical realisation among different institutional players into concrete action, by bringing them together in practice. In other words, the third political objective of the EUGS was to act as a bureaucratic silo-breaking exercise, and through the breaking or at least the bending of silos, contribute to better policy outcomes which the Union badly needed. The strategic reflection and the EUGS sought to live up to up the letter and spirit of the Lisbon Treaty, which was far from being fully implemented as far as the Union's external action is concerned.

The three political aims underpinning the EUGS—policy direction, political unity and a joined-up Union—were strictly connected, for good and ill. On the one hand, a vicious circle could clearly be traced: the multiple crises had led the Union to lose its bearings, as well as causing or exacerbating multiple divisions between and within the Member States and the EU institutions. These divisions fed and fuelled siloed policy responses, which were woefully inadequate to tackle the multiple crises that spread and deepened by the day. On the other hand, the strategic reflection and the EUGS sought to make one small step to reverse the trend into a more virtuous dynamic. A shared narrative could at once provide a sense of direction to navigate the multiple crises surrounding the EU and contribute to healing the manifold divisions within it. Such healing would in turn contribute to the breaking of policy and institutional silos and thus seek to deliver more effective policy necessary to address the manifold crises.

With this political rationale in mind, the process, the content and the follow-up of the EUGS had to be shaped accordingly, much like the political rationale for the ESS had framed the 2003 and 2008 endeavours.

Notes

1. Cameron opened the campaign by saying that the EU was vital for the UK's security, making many think that he was going to make a broad case for Remain; strangely he then switched to making exclusively the economic case for staying in, and stayed there throughout the campaign.
2. Among such exceptions, it is worth recalling the attention devoted by HRVP Ashton to revising the European Neighbourhood Policy in 2011. Today, the 2011 revision of the ENP is considered a failure, triggering a further revision in 2015. But at the time, when hopes for an Arab spring ran high, the 2011 revision was cautiously welcomed by many (Cassarino and Tocci 2011).

References

Balfour, Rosa. 2014. *Renewal Through International Action? Options for EU Foreign Policy*. Brussels: European Policy Centre. http://www.epc.eu/documents/uploads/pub_4951_balfour.pdf.

Cassarino, Jean-Pierre, and Nathalie Tocci. 2011. *Rethinking the EU's Mediterranean Policies Post-9/11*. IAI Working Papers No. 11/6. Rome: IAI. http://www.iai.it/en/node/3302.

Devrim, Deniz, and Evelina Schulz. 2009. *Enlargement Fatigue in the European Union: From Enlargement to Many Unions*. Elcano Working Paper No. 13/2009. Madrid: Real Istituto Elcano. http://www.realinstitutoelcano.org/wps/portal/web/rielcano_en/contenido?WCM_GLOBAL_CONTEXT=/elcano/elcano_in/zonas_in/DT13-2009.

EU High Representative. 2003. *A Secure Europe in a Better World. European Security Strategy*. December. https://www.consilium.europa.eu/uedocs/cmsUpload/78367.pdf.

Henry, Giulia, and Ferruccio Pastore. 2014. *The Governance of Migration, Mobility and Asylum in the EU: A Contentious Laboratory*. Imagining Europe Working Paper No. 5. Rome: IAI. http://www.iai.it/en/node/1862.

Juncker, Jean-Claude, et al. 2015. *Completing Europe's Economic and Monetary Union*. Brussels, June.https://ec.europa.eu/priorities/sites/beta-political/files/5-presidents-report_en.pdf.

Pew Research Center. 2016. Europeans Face the World Divided. Pew Survey, June. http://pewrsr.ch/1WIdvUf.

Schmidt, Vivien A. 2013. Democracy and Legitimacy in the European Union Revisited: Input, Output and 'Throughput'. *Political Studies* 61 (1): 2–22. doi: 10.1111/j.1467-9248.2012.00962.x.

Schmidt, Vivien. 2016. *The New EU Governance: New Intergovernmentalism, New Supranationalism, and New Parliamentarism*. IAI Working Papers No. 16/11. Rome: IAI. http://www.iai.it/en/node/6311.

The White House. 2002. *National Security Strategy of the United States of America*. Washington DC, September. http://www.state.gov/documents/organization/63562.pdf.

Tsoukalis, Loukas. 2016. *In Defence of Europe: Can the European Project Be Saved?* Oxford: Oxford University Press.

Van Rompuy, Herman, et al. 2012. *Towards a Genuine Economic and Monetary Union*. Brussels, 5 December.http://www.consilium.europa.eu/uedocs/cms_Data/docs/pressdata/en/ec/134069.pdf.

CHAPTER 3

How to Make a Strategy?

It took almost 2 years to produce the EU Global Strategy. Clearly, it does not take 2 years to produce a policy document. What happened in that period? How was the process of EU strategic reflection organised in order to build a consensus within, between and beyond the official institutions and the Member States? What lessons were learned from the previous strategy-making experiences: the 2003 European Security Strategy and the 2008 Implementation Report? How were these applied as the HRVP and her team moved forward in this work? And what does this process tell us about EU foreign policy making more broadly?

STRATEGY-MAKING IN 2003 AND 2008: THE LESSONS LEARNED

The lessons drawn from the processes followed in 2003 and in 2008 for devising the ESS and the Implementation Report, respectively, were important. Those two exercises, in different ways, pointed to the same hard truth: it is highly unlikely that the EU can produce a Strategy which is readable, fairly concise, avoids bureaucratic jargon and coherent in terms of structure, style and content by following traditional procedures. If a draft is produced through traditional channels, going through the steamroller of comments, track changes and suggestions by all the Member States and EU institutions, the result is as far from strategy as imaginable. Consensus within the EU is possible if everything that is

© The Author(s) 2017   29
N. Tocci, *Framing the EU Global Strategy*, Palgrave Studies
in European Union Politics, DOI 10.1007/978-3-319-55586-7_3

objectionable to anyone is removed and everything which is important to someone is included. One only needs to read Council conclusions to see how the result generally takes the form of highly diluted and poorly "actionable" shopping lists of views, goals and, rarely, proposed actions. Council conclusions serve important purposes. Strategy is not one of them.

Javier Solana knew this well in 2003. The idea of producing a European Security Strategy was first aired by then German Foreign Minister Joschka Fischer at an informal Foreign Affairs Council meeting—known as Gymnich—held on the Greek island of Kastellòrizo after the end of Operation Iraqi Freedom in May 2003. HR Solana promptly acted upon the suggestion, and in little over a month, the document was ready. *A Secure Europe in a Better World* was submitted to and welcomed by the European Council meeting in Thessaloniki on 20 June 2003. To be fair, that version of the ESS was not endorsed by the European Council. The Thessaloniki European Council tasked Solana to "bring this work forward, to further examine our security challenges [...] with a view to submitting an EU Security Strategy [...] to be adopted by the European Council in December" (European Council 2003). Indeed, Solana and his team further revised the text in the months that followed, and the final version was adopted by the European Council in December 2003.

HR Solana produced a focused and compelling text in a tight time frame of little over 6 months. To do so, he set up a small team under his personal guidance. The "pen" was held firmly in the hands of a very few, notably Robert Cooper, the Director General for Security and Defence Policy in the Council General Secretariat, and Christoph Heusgen, Head of the Policy Unit of the Council. In fact, the ESS was anecdotally drafted by Cooper over a week-end. The Member States and EU institutions, of course, were not completely cut-off. A key event in the process was a meeting of European Political Directors, who had been far more involved in the discussions over the Iraq war than the Member States' representatives in Brussels. In addition, the Political and Security Committee (PSC) held a couple of dedicated meetings on the text, and all the Member States plus the 10 soon-to-be members which were already fully associated with the Common Foreign and Security Policy (CFSP) were invited to submit written contributions on the basis of the June version of the text. Not all the Member States and candidate countries contributed, and those that did displayed widely different degrees of engagement in the exercise. Broadly speaking, however, all the Member States, including the most engaged, allowed the HR wide space for manoeuvre and initiative. In fact, while being born from within the institutions, the document was not negotiated nor drafted by committee, be it in the working groups, in the Committee of Permanent Representatives (COREPER) or in PSC.

A focused outreach and consultation process beyond official institutions was organised in parallel. Under the directorship of Nicole Gnesotto, the EU Institute for Security Studies (EUISS) organised three expert seminars on the three main sections of the June version of the ESS—the security environment, strategic objectives and policy implications—in Rome (September), Paris and Stockholm (October), respectively, in partnership with national think tanks.

The procedure followed in 2008 bore some similarities with 2003, but also some important differences with it. As in 2003, the pen was held firmly by the Policy Unit of the Council, this time under the leadership of Helga Schmid. But the Member States were included far more organically in the exercise. Rather than only a couple of meetings with PSC, the Implementation Report was the subject of several formal and informal meetings over the course of 2008, including with PSC and security policy directors, under the aegis of the Slovenian and French rotating presidencies. Successive drafts of the Report were sent to the 27 Member States, although without entering into a line-by-line drafting by committee, at least in theory. Unlike the 2003 ESS, the 2008 Implementation Report was also presented and discussed in the European Parliament's foreign affairs committee, and the European Commission. Notably the Directorate General for External Relations (known as DG Relex at the time) within the Commission was closely involved in the exercise. As in 2003, the EUISS was involved also in 2008, organising four seminars in Rome, Warsaw, Helsinki and Paris, again in collaboration with national think tanks.

The similarities and differences between the procedures used for the ESS and the Implementation Report had an impact on the respective contents. The ESS was short, crisp and highly readable, providing the EU with the first strategic vision for its role in the world. It did not, however, propose concrete actions to take the EU there. Indeed, HR Solana was never keen on calling it a Strategy, a title Member States added at a later stage. Hence, while the ESS was adopted by the European Council, it did not expressly commit the Member States to a specific set of actions, nor did it commit to action the European Commission which was largely kept out of the exercise. In 2008, a somewhat more formal procedure was followed. There was a deeper and broader engagement with both the Member States and with the European Parliament and the Commission. While in principle the text was not negotiated, in practice when successive drafts were circulated to the Member States and the institutions, a negotiation by default tended to be the outcome. The result was a far longer and less incisive document, which continued to meet the resistance of some Member States on specific bits of wording. Hence, the document was only broadly supported rather than endorsed by the Council in December that year. However, the Implementation Report was more comprehensive and "actionable" than the 2003 ESS, which essentially provided a broad strategic concept for the EU. Finally, neither in the case of the ESS nor of the Implementation Report was there an extensive process of external consultation. In both cases, the EUISS organised a handful of expert seminars as a complement to official procedures rather than as a self-standing dimension of the process in its own right. The main goal was that of seeking agreement within the Council, notably between the three largest Member States. A broad consultation process was deemed unnecessary.

From these two precedents, important lessons were drawn by HRVP Mogherini and her team. Particularly from the 2003 ESS, we understood that formal procedures could not be followed. Had we done so, the result would certainly not have been a readable and incisive document. The higher degree of institutionalisation in the process used in 2008 compared to 2003 was clearly visible in the content of the text and in its reception by the Council. But to be fair, already in 2008, the EU was a far more complex animal, having almost doubled in size compared with 2003, and being on the verge of making an institutional leap forward through what was to become the Lisbon Treaty in 2009. As such, simply repeating the extremely light institutional touch of 2003 would not have been possible in 2008; less still was it an option in 2015–2016. The Member States would have to be involved far more systematically in 2015–2016, along with a systematic involvement of the Commission. Since the 2010s, a renationalisation of foreign policy has been under way. It is difficult to imagine the Member States in the 2010s entrusting the freedom of manoeuvre to the HR which Solana enjoyed in 2003. Likewise, the Commission had to be involved because, unlike in 2003, the Lisbon Treaty was in force bringing together the Common Foreign and Security

Policy within the Council and the external relations of the Commission, with the European External Action Service acting as the glue in between. Finally, unlike both 2003 and 2008, external outreach and consultation in 2015–2016 could not simply be considered a nice-but-not-essential ornament: given the sorry state of the Union in 2015–2016, a far broader and deeper outreach and consultation process was necessary. The HRVP, her team and EU institutions more broadly had to make a far greater effort at public diplomacy than was the case in past exercises.

FIRST STEPS

The seeds of the EUGS were sown in October 2014 during Federica Mogherini's hearing at the European Parliament as the designated candidate for the post of HRVP, taking over from her predecessor Catherine Ashton. On that occasion, Federica put down the first marker, calling for a "strategic rethink" in EU foreign policy, after 11 years since the first and only European Security Strategy was produced by HR Solana (Mogherini 2014). She did not delve into the details at that time, but the first seeds of what was to become the EU strategic reflection process were sown back then.

The actual work began in early January 2015, in the light of the looming deadline deriving from the mandate entrusted to the HRVP by the European Council in December 2013. In those European Council conclusions, the HRVP was tasked "in close cooperation with the Commission, to assess the impact of changes in the global environment, and to report to the Council in the course of 2015 on the challenges and opportunities arising for the Union, following consultations with the Member States" (European Council 2013).

By her 100th day in office, on the occasion of the 51st Munich Security Conference in February 2015, Mogherini expressed the clear intention of producing a new strategy: "We need a sense of direction. We need an ability to make choices and to prioritize. We need a sense of how we can best mobilize our instruments to serve our goals and in partnership with whom….We need a new strategy". Her rationale was clear: "In these times of crisis it is not easy to go beyond the immediacy of today. But taking the time to look ahead is not a luxury. It is an essential prerequisite to transition from the current global chaos to a new peaceful global order" (Mogherini 2015). While she always made clear to me that an EU strategy should not be an action plan, it should nonetheless provide the EU and its Member States with a common sense of strategic direction that would ultimately guide action.

In other words, the broad intention was clear early on. However, the process had to be invented from scratch and had to be fit for purpose. What was obvious from the outset was that the HRVP could not replicate the same method used in 2003. A process of European strategic reflection in 2015–2016 could look nothing like what it did in the early 2000s. We live in a different Union, a different world. As discussed in Chap. 1, in 2003 HR Solana set up a small team, which worked on a draft over the course of several weeks, organised a handful of seminars in different European capitals and discussed the draft ESS with political directors and in a few sessions of the PSC before the document was adopted by the European Council. The ESS provided the Union with its first strategic vision, which helped mend the intra-European and transatlantic rift over the 2003 war in Iraq. It did not, however, indicate the means to achieve this vision.

In 2016, a radically different approach was needed and had to respond to the two principal purposes of an eventual strategy: a shared vision and common action. On the one hand, the Union needed a new shared vision that would provide a sense of policy direction and heal divisions regarding its role in the world, as discussed in Chap. 2. But unlike 2003, in 2015–2016 there was not one single cleavage which a shared narrative had to reconcile: there were several and overlapping rifts between and within the Member States and EU institutions. As far as foreign policy is concerned, the main cleavages to be bridged were on migration, Russia and the role of European defence. The solidity of the European project risked being shaken by these interlocking foreign policy cleavages, compounding the even more acute divisions over economic governance and asylum as discussed in Chap. 2.

On the other hand, a vision alone, while sufficient in 2003 when Europe had never been "so prosperous, so secure, nor so free" (EU HR 2003: 1), would have been inadequate in 2016. The EU is undergoing multiple threats and challenges, but can also seize the unprecedented opportunities deriving from new technologies and the incipient digital age. To confront the challenges and seize the opportunities, credible, responsive and joined-up common action is of the essence. An EU Global Strategy, therefore, had to be "actionable": it could not limit itself to the shared vision, but had to point the way forward regarding the common action.

A Two-Phase Process of Strategic Reflection

The HRVP began with what she had: the mandate from the December 2013 European Council inviting the High Representative to produce an assessment of the changing global environment and the challenges and opportunities this implied for the EU.

In January 2015, the HRVP decided to divide the process into two phases. In the first phase, running from January to June 2015, the work would concentrate on producing a strategic assessment as requested by the European Council in 2013 (see Annex A). If the European Council would give the HRVP a mandate to pursue the work further, a second phase would then concentrate on the Strategy proper (see Annex B). Five reasons underpinned this move.

First, the mandate. The December 2013 European Council did give the HRVP a mandate, but it was not a mandate to produce a new Strategy. The wording of those conclusions reflected what at the time was an ambiguous position within the European Council on the subject. As discussed in Chap. 1, since 2008 there had been several attempts to relaunch an EU strategic debate. But a critical mass of the Member States in favour of a new strategy struggled to emerge. As the Eurozone crisis raged on, precious little attention was paid to EU strategy-making in the turbulent years that followed. By 2013, the European Council, amidst a rapidly deteriorating security environment, agreed on a fudge: it mandated the HRVP not to deliver a new European Security Strategy, but to "do something" about strategy by producing a report on the changes in the global environment and the challenges and opportunities arising for the Union (European Council 2013). The HRVP had to fulfil the letter of that mandate. This she set out to do.

Beyond this, however, Federica's intent was that of obtaining an explicit mandate for a new Strategy. By devoting a first phase of the work to producing a strategic assessment and presenting it to the European Council, the aim was to obtain from the latter a specific tasking for developing a Strategy proper. The goal was accomplished, with the European Council in June 2015 stating that: "the High Representative will continue the process of strategic reflection with a view to preparing an EU Global Strategy on foreign and security policy in close cooperation with Member States, to be submitted to the European Council by June 2016" (European Council 2015).

Second, the timing. Some, both within and outside EU institutions, had suggested that the December 2013 European Council conclusions could have been read as a mandate for a new Strategy. While this was dubious at best, truth is that the new HRVP was in no rush. Had the December 2013 conclusions been interpreted as a mandate to produce a new Strategy, then by December 2015 at the latest,[1] little over a year into the new job, Federica Mogherini would have had to deliver. It is certainly possible to write a document, even a good one, in 1 year. But can a new HRVP settle into a new job, manage the urgency of the day of which there are many, define her priorities, make the necessary institutional adjustments to reflect these, and build trust, momentum and convergence among the 28 Member States, EU institutions and the wider foreign policy community on a major strategic document in that lapse of time? Probably not.

Added to this, it is worth recalling the political context in which Federica Mogherini had been appointed as HRVP. At the nadir of relations between the EU and Russia, following Russia's annexation of Crimea, the destabilisation of eastern Ukraine, and the downing of MH17, as a former Italian Foreign Minister, Mogherini was suspected by several Member States, notably in central and eastern Europe, of being too soft on Russia. Her appointment had been contested and suspicions about her among some Member States took some time to die down. On top came the criticisms in the summer of 2014 concerning her relative youth and inexperience, shared at the time by many establishment elites across the Union.[2] In such a context, stretching—and to some extent twisting—a mandate to produce a mere assessment of the strategic environment into one developing a new Strategy would have been a step too far.

And Federica Mogherini was in no hurry. To her, the process was always supposed to be as if not more important than the product itself, a point that she repeatedly made in her public speeches. In Munich in February 2015, she called for a strategy "that is not drawn up in a closet by a select few, but a broad process that involves the Member States and EU institutions, as well as the foreign policy community spanning across academic and think tanks, the media and civil society" (Mogherini 2015). She meant what she said. This was not out of political correctness, but because if a strategy—regardless of its quality—is to provide a reference point for foreign policy-makers and shapers across the Union, rather than becoming a dust-collecting document lying on a few desks, it must be the product of a collective rethink. And this takes time. Hence, the rationale of dividing the exercise into two phases. By June, we aimed to produce a "strategic assessment" following the letter of the December 2013 conclusions, hoping that this would provide the springboard to move forward on the Strategy proper.

Third, the need to clear the ground in the strategic reflection. Dividing the process of strategic reflection into two phases made sense analytically. An assessment of the strategic environment is the ground zero of a strategy. It is the snapshot of the world, and how it is expected to evolve, that informs ensuing policy action: it is the diagnosis that precedes the prognosis. The picture painted by the assessment is of a fundamentally changed strategic environment. In 2003, the international liberal order seemed unchallenged—9/11 notwithstanding—and the EU's soft power was at its peak with the eastern enlargement approaching the finishing line and the ENP in the offing. By 2015 that world was gone. The strategic assessment described the world as more connected, contested and complex. The world has become more connected, with greater connectivity in terms of movement of persons, economic interdependence and communication technology, bringing about both challenges and opportunities (see Annex A: 104-107). The world has become more contested, notably within the EU and its surrounding regions to the east and south, but also as a result of climate change and the growing competition over natural resources (see Annex A: 107-111). And the world has become more complex, with power shifting from west to east but also diffusing beyond state boundaries (see Annex A: 111-115; also Howorth 2016). These three "C's" apply both within and beyond the EU and are intimately related. Greater contestation within the EU, in its surrounding regions and in the broader global order, is the results of greater connectivity and globalisation as well as of greater complexity and the power shifts and temporary power vacuums it is generating. An assessment of these fundamental changes was the necessary baseline for the Strategy. By getting the assessment out, we aimed to clear the ground of all description and analysis that would have otherwise found its way into the Strategy proper. Having cleared that ground, the Global Strategy could be just that: a strategy.

Fourth, the strategic assessment served to set markers for the ensuing Strategy. Through the scope of the strategic assessment, the HRVP indicated her intention to engage in this process by using to the full her hats as High Representative of the Union for Foreign Affairs and Security Policy as well as Vice-President of the European Commission. The seeds for this approach, which ultimately blossomed in the Strategy proper, were sown in the December 2013 European Council conclusions mandating the strategic assessment. In those conclusions, the European Council called for the assessment to be made by the HRVP "in close cooperation with the Commission" (European Council 2013). This could be read as implying that the policy areas that it would cover should also include those falling under the competences of the Commission. Indeed, the strategic assessment in its final section reviewed the pros and cons of all the EU's external action instruments, including not only diplomacy, security and defence falling within the remit of the HR, but the full range of external action instruments, including trade, development, humanitarian assistance, energy, climate, research, education, migration and mobility, falling under the hat of VP (see Annex A: 120-124). By assessing the full range of external instruments and policies in the strategic assessment, the expectation it generated was that in the second phase dedicated to developing a Strategy proper, the full range of policies and instruments would be factored in.

Fifth, the two-staged process served to test a working method. Given the value attached to the strategic reflection, dividing it up into two phases allowed the HRVP to develop a working method, and build trust, consensus and momentum for the second and more complicated phase devoted to the Strategy proper. In the 6 months of work on the strategic assessment between January and June 2015, we developed a tailor-made process of strategy-making through a trial and error run to see what worked and what did not, allowing the HRVP to recalibrate the process for the second phase aimed at developing the Strategy itself. In those first 6 months, we established an informal small working group including officials from the European External Action Service, the European Commission, the Council Secretariat and the European Council. We held regular meetings with the EEAS Secretary General and Senior Management. We reached out to representatives of the Commission, notably those engaged in sectoral strategic projects in 2015 such as the European Neighbourhood Policy review, the 2015 Trade Strategy, the Agenda on Migration and the Energy Union. It was essential that the strategic assessment, that talked the talk of the end of silos in favour of a more joined-up EU, also walked the walk by joining-up with other strategic exercises underway in the Brussels beltway. As regards Member States, we engaged at various levels, notably with policy planners, while keeping the PSC and COREPER, and naturally the Foreign Affairs Council duly informed. Broadening out beyond official

players, the EUISS organised a major conference in April 2015 in which
the draft outline of the strategic assessment was presented and the HRVP
engaged in a long Q&A session with an expert audience.

As the weeks went by, the HRVP understood what worked and
what did not. The Strategic Planning division within the EEAS was a
key asset in this process, as was the input of the top management of
the EEAS. The EUISS played a valuable role and was the natural hub
to coordinate the public outreach and consultation dimension of the
strategic reflection. By contrast, we learnt that the Member States
had to be included in the process in a far more systematic way so as
to ensure their buy-into the process and the document. However, this
did not mean engaging only with the existing working bodies of the
Council. Member State buy-in required very regular and lengthy meetings, and neither COREPER nor PSC would have had sufficient time
for this exercise. We also understood that the Commission's contribution, while coordinated by the Secretariat General, required direct input
from the various Directorates General (DGs), beginning with those falling under the Commissioners' Group on External Action—i.e. trade,
development, humanitarian assistance, enlargement and neighbourhood
policy—and moving beyond them to include mobility, transport, migration, energy, climate, research, education, growth and employment
among others.

Over the first 6 months, consensus between the Member States on
the desirability of moving forward on a strategy crystallised and con-
solidated. While from 2008 to 2013 there was a division between the
Member States regarding an EU Global Strategy, by 2015 all agreed that
the security environment had so radically changed—and not for the better—that a strategic rethink was imperative.

TOWARDS A COMMON NARRATIVE

Having completed the first phase of the work in June 2015 with the
presentation of the strategic assessment, the work on the Strategy proper
began in September 2015. It was designed to have two principal dimensions: a public outreach and consultation dimension, and an official and
institutional dimension. When it came to the former, we were particularly inspired by the 2014 "German review": a review of German foreign
policy which, while not having a national security strategy as its outcome,
had led to an extremely rich and innovative process of self-reflection

within the *Auswärtiges Amt*, the German federal foreign ministry. While in the EU's case the output was a strategy, Federica Mogherini's emphasis on the need for a broad and inclusive reflection process required a specific design for that purpose. If one of the basic purposes of the EUGS was to forge a common narrative on foreign and security policy among Europeans, which would help bridge over difference and spark a debate within the European foreign policy community on the EU's role in the world, it could not be a strategy cooked up in a room by one or two people. It had to be the product of a collective effort, which would place the Member States and EU institutions at the centre, but which aimed to reach out beyond them, including universities and students, think tanks and civil society organisations, social actors and the private sector, as well as countries and organisations beyond the EU's borders.

Public Outreach and Consultation

The advice and prediction of a diplomat who had been at the forefront of the German foreign policy review was well received and turned out to be correct. He suggested that so long as we put in place a basic skeleton of activities, much more would be tagged on as the process acquired momentum. This was what had happened in the case of the German review, and it was likely that the same dynamic would unfold at EU level. And it did. Back in the summer of 2015 when the 5–6 people engaged in this endeavour—the HRVP, and several colleagues from her Cabinet, the Strategic Planning Division of the EEAS, the EUISS, and I—had started brainstorming about how to organise the process and present ideas to the HRVP, we had imagined approximately 6–8 conferences in different capitals on different themes—be these geographic or thematic—connected to the Strategy. This was more than double what had been done in 2003, but indeed the EU at 28 Member States had almost doubled in size since the EU-15 of 2003. These would be co-organised by the EUISS in partnership with different national think tanks or universities and with the support of a private foundation. Following the EUISS's opening conference of the outreach and consultation process in October 2015, the fall of 2015 saw the organisation of the first handful of such events.

Between then and the end of the consultation process in April 2016, the list ballooned. The bulk of the outreach effort was within the EU. It was, after all, an EU strategic reflection process aimed at producing an EU Global Strategy. It was within the EU itself that convergence and ultimately consensus had to be forged through a dialogue which should be as inclusive as possible. In the end, over 50 events were organised across the EU on the EUGS.[3] All Member State foreign ministries co-organised at least one such event, which normally saw the participation of that Member State's foreign minister or defence minister—and in one case the Head of state—and was carried out together with a national think tank or university. Several think tanks and NGOs organised their events independently, be it in Brussels or elsewhere.

A more limited but meaningful effort was made to reach out beyond the EU. At the EEAS's Heads of Delegation conference in September 2015, the HRVP launched the second phase of the strategic reflection and invited delegations to play an active role in it. We travelled to the USA, Japan, Brazil, Australia, Norway, Georgia and Serbia, seeking to balance the emphasis between the EU's global and its regional roles. We also arranged several meetings with UN and NATO officials over the course of the consultation. The list of extra-EU events was patchy as the core of the work was intra-EU. But it was nonetheless important to discuss and consult with the outside world, above all listening to their perceptions of the EU and what its role in the world should be.

Beyond these events, we received a wealth of written contributions and established a dedicated website for the process.[4] The EUISS invited 50 experts, 30 of which were from the EU and 20 from elsewhere to provide opinion pieces (Missiroli 2016). Alongside, we organised a student essay competition, and the HRVP engaged with a group of Erasmus alumni over the themes of the EUGS. A wide range of players made their voice heard: from human rights NGOs to defence industry associations, and from trade unions to the Catholic Church. I was personally surprised by the degree of interest this process solicited from very different walks of European political life.

Back in 2003 when Solana and his team worked on the ESS, an effort of this kind was probably unnecessary. The purpose of the exercise in 2003 was that of rekindling the official lines of France and Germany on the one hand and the UK on the other after the war in Iraq. The process was rightly designed to serve that purpose: it did not require a massive outreach and consultation effort. In 2016, the EUGS was being developed amidst multiple and overlapping cleavages between the 28 Member States, be these of a strictly internal nature—economic governance—at the nexus of internal and external policies—migration—or foreign policy—Russia. Moreover, the Strategy was being crafted in a climate of growing populist Euroscepticism across the Union. It is a climate in which the old narrative underpinning the European project—peace on the continent—no longer has traction among the younger generations. It is a context in which globalisation and interdependence, which lie at the core of European integration, are deeply contested by majorities or large minorities in many Member States and beyond. In other words, the idealistic narrative of Europe as a peace project is dimming, while the utilitarian narrative of Europe as a luxury has been seriously compromised by the economic crisis and the growing disaffection of the losers of globalisation in the Western world, including Europe. But the truth is that in a more connected and complex world, the EU is a necessity: only continental-sized powers can hope to wield influence in the twenty-first century and seize the opportunities and confront the challenges that the world presents.

In this climate, foreign policy offers a narrow opening to rekindle some Europeans to the European project. Foreign policy remains the area in which the European citizens demand more Europe. A 2016 Pew Research Center survey found that 74% of Europeans would like to see a stronger EU role in the world. This included British citizens, 55% of whom supported the proposition (Pew Research Center 2016: 5). Moreover, while foreign policy remains on the margins of the European public space, issues that touch the daily lives of Europeans in fact often have external origins, be it terrorism, energy insecurity and irregular migration, or are transnational by definition such as climate change and the economic insecurity unleashed by globalisation. The short-term responses sought to these challenges are local, national or intra-European. But to address them effectively, the Union and its Member States must lift their gaze and engage the wider world. This was the reflection made by the mayor of a European city during the strategic reflection, who pointed out to me that in his daily work he only had the competences to firefight the symptoms of a long list of challenges, whose causes could only be addressed through an effective foreign policy broadly construed.

To be fair, foreign policy is unlikely to be the policy area that will re-enamour the masses with the EU. Foreign policy is and is likely to remain an interest for a relatively small segment of the European—and non-European—populace. Especially among officials, I often heard the plea to write a strategy in a language that would be read and understood by ordinary European citizens. That the utmost effort had to be made to avoid bureaucratic jargon and reach out as widely as possible to the public was imperative. But to believe or expect the Global Strategy to be read by each and every citizen was somewhat naïve. In some respect, I thought it was a sad symptom of how detached some elites are from ordinary citizens if they genuinely think that a document such as the EU Global Strategy, readable and accessible as it sought to be, would be read by the man and woman in the street. As a little experiment during the drafting phase, I asked a close friend, a teacher in a music conservatory in southern Italy, to read the text. She reached the end of the document, but admittedly struggled. And I would not even claim that she represents the average European, as a well-travelled and highly educated professional. She simply works in a field which is unrelated to the EU and foreign policy. All this to say that while the ambition to reach the "ordinary citizen" always struck me as a symptom of the other-worldliness of some officials and experts, to the extent that there is a segment of the population that does care about foreign policy, that community had to be actively engaged. It is a community that does not comprise only governments, diplomats and officials, but also students and academics, NGOs and think tanks, journalists and bloggers, trade unions and business associations. The strategic reflection's outreach and consultation effort sought to reach out to that community. The acknowledgements in the annex of the EUGS list all those who contributed to the effort over the course of the strategic reflection. I have been too close to the process to judge whether the effort made was sufficient or not. Readers themselves will be far better judges than me.

Member States and EU Institutions

The content and eventually the wording of the EUGS had to be discussed in depth within the official institutions and the Member States as the core stakeholders of the exercise. As mentioned above, a genuine buy-in from the Member States required their substantive and sustained input over the months. Neither COREPER nor PSC were likely to commit in practice. We, therefore, chose a different method, asking the Member States to appoint the points of contact (POC) with whom we would engage in monthly meetings about the EUGS. Alongside, the Secretariat General of the Commission established a task force of officials representing the external dimensions of their respective DGs. Almost all DGs were involved in the taskforce.

Together with the POCs and the Commission taskforce, we discussed, chapter by chapter, the EUGS over the course of 9 months.
Having agreed on a broad outline of the document by December 2015,
we distributed a set of questionnaires to the Member States and the
Commission reflecting the main priorities that we intended to cover
in the EUGS. We did so partly because several non-papers, particularly from the Member States, were already beginning to flow in. If left
undirected, the risk was that this input would have been of limited use.
We, therefore, chose to steer the input by providing specific questions
to the Member States and the Commission. We did so also because we
genuinely needed their contribution. In order to produce an analytically coherent document, the general skeleton had to be elaborated top-
down, and this we did. But the flesh on the bones could not come from
a handful of people. It could only become a meaningful Strategy through
the substantive input of all those stakeholders working daily on the various dimensions of the EU's external action across all capitals.

When explaining the working method, we invited the Member States
and the Commission to be as innovative as possible: to imagine what the
EU could and should do, not today or tomorrow, but in 5, 6 or 7 years.
On occasions, I was baffled by the response. In some cases, rather than
responding to the questions, I received track changes to the formulation
of questions themselves: officials, particularly in multilateral contexts, have
developed a chronic track change syndrome. On other occasions the invitation to be creative left officials feeling uncomfortable. One day during a
meeting, upon my invitation to "think outside the box", one participant
replied "Nathalie, we cannot think outside the box. We are the box!".

To be fair, though, the response from both the Member States and
the Commission was extremely rich and rewarding. While the outline
of the Strategy and its driving philosophy came from the HRVP and
her team, the actual content came from the Member States and the
Commission, alongside the input from the wider foreign policy community through the public outreach and consultation. As Robert Cooper
told me when reminiscing about his role in 2003, I also regarded myself
as the secretary, articulating as clearly as possible what the Member States
and the Commission wanted to say, and how the HRVP interpreted it.
When drafting the Strategy, I relied on a few simple criteria to decide
what to insert and what not. I tried to discern those areas in which
there was a critical mass of support from the Member States and the
Commission. A strong stance on security and defence or a prioritisation

of the EU's action in the neighbouring eastern and southern regions were the two key examples. I selected other ideas from the individual Member States, which seemed original and would not meet the opposition of the others. Specific issues such as ocean governance, strategic communications, cyber security, post-conflict stabilisation or the reform of multilateral institutions are all cases in point.

When I could, I tried to stick to the actual wording used in the non-papers sent to us. This was a good piece of advice I received from one of the drafters of the 2015 US National Security Strategy during a visit to Washington in the fall of 2015. When I asked him for some tips on how to manage the process, he suggested that when possible I should use the exact bits of wording I received from the various contributions. Those who contributed would read themselves somewhere in the Strategy, and this would likely increase their support for it. I am 100% sure that all those who contributed to the strategic reflection, both from within and outside the official institutions, in reading carefully the EUGS will find themselves reflected somewhere in the text.

I learnt, however, that the Member States' buy-in required more than the regular interaction with the POCs. This was not least for reasons related to institutional hierarchy: their institutional superiors wanted to have a direct word. As the weeks went by, many wanted to have a say, and the Dutch EU Presidency, one of the key allies in this process, was eager to arrange such opportunities. In early 2016, the EUGS was discussed with the Member States at different levels: political directors, security directors, defence directors, secretaries general of ministries of foreign affairs, the PSC, the EU Military Committee, the Politico-Military Group, as well as by the Foreign Affairs Council, the informal Defence Council and the Development Council. The EUGS was also subject of debate by the European Parliament, which produced its own report on the Strategy (European Parliament 2016), and was discussed by the inter-parliamentary conference with delegates from the Member States' national parliaments. Several national parliaments also passed dedicated resolutions as their own input into the process.

In full honesty, the purpose of this plethora of meetings was less to contribute to the fine details of the EUGS and more to ensure the widest possible inclusion from the Member States and EU institutions, and therefore their buy-into the process and eventually the product. My main interlocutors from the Member States were the POCs alongside the Commission task force with whom I had the opportunity to meet regularly and therefore engage in detailed discussion on substance, and towards the end of the process, on the fine wording of the text itself. But while the content was the key, political and institutional support required this much broader effort.

The breadth and depth of the official involvement in the strategic reflection was the key to galvanise the Member States' and EU institutions' support. This was necessary, in turn, to make sure the EU Global Strategy succeeded in tackling head on, and not skirting around, the perennial points of contestation in the European foreign policy debate. Be these about the role of European defence, NATO, about relations with Russia, or about the increasingly salient role of migration in the EU's external action, the Strategy had to provide guidance, which had at once to be substantive as well as shared by all. This required countless meetings and long hours of discussion. These discussions went on until the evening of the 25th June, minutes before the EUGS was formally circulated to the Member States. I recall the nonchalant way in which the Member States at the beginning of the process had conscientiously agreed that the EUGS should not be subject to a line-by-line negotiation. In retrospect, I wonder what it would have been like had they advanced such a demand at the outset, considering that we ended up poring over every word and comma of the text. But in hindsight, had this not been done, we would have ended up at best with an unwieldy and incoherent Christmas tree: a long shopping list without much analytical clarity, prioritisation and strategic intent. This was one of the lessons learned from the 2008 Implementation Report on the ESS, which had gone through endless toing and froing in the PSC, the outcome of which was far from stellar. At worst, we would have had no Strategy at all. In short, the long, intense and yes, at times repetitive, meetings with the widest possible set of players were critical to achieving a Strategy which was just that: a strategy.

A DRAMATIC FINALE

The last stretch of the EU strategic reflection coincided with the referendum campaign in the UK on British membership in the European Union. The looming referendum was front and centre in the minds of most of my interlocutors. On the one hand, all realised how important it was to avoid becoming caught up and instrumentalised in the haywire referendum campaign in the UK. The myths sold in that campaign are subject of a different book. Suffice it to say here that of the many lies told, there was also an allegedly "top secret plan"—the EUGS—to set up an EU army (Waterfield 2016). Whereas the EUGS made no such claims, a leaked quote could have been twisted to that effect.

But the deeper question connecting the UK referendum and the EU Global Strategy was whether and how the result of the vote would have changed the decision to proceed or otherwise with the Strategy, which was due to be presented to the European Council 5 days after the UK vote, on the 28th June. In the months leading to the UK referendum, my hunch was that in the event of a Remain vote in the UK on 23 June 2016, we would have circulated officially the EUGS the following day for it to be formally presented by the HRVP to the European Council on 28 June 2016. The time frame was tight and meant that the Member States would not have had the time for proper deliberation and consultations within their national institutions. This posed a problem for several Member States, whose domestic legislation obliges the government to consult parliament before formally giving its blessing to a document such as the EUGS. This meant that the European Council would not have been in the position to "endorse" or "adopt" the Strategy, a term with strong connotations in Eurocratese. Nor could the HRVP have lived with the European Council merely "taking note" of the EUGS, another Euro-term whose translation amounts to an explicit political distancing from the object in question. The most we could extract was for the European Council to "welcome the presentation of the EUGS". It was not ideal, particularly considering that by the end of the process of informal negotiations, every Member State had agreed with every word of the EUGS, but circumstances were exceptional and the HRVP was determined to press ahead. If instead the British public would have voted Leave, then the situation would have drastically changed. Up until the 23rd June, my understanding was that the HRVP would have held back, postponing the EUGS to a later date.

When the shocking news of Brexit hit home around 5 am on the 24th, I assumed it would all be called off. Indeed, this was the HRVP's first inclination that day. Yet as the hours went by, it became increasingly clear that presenting the EUGS in September was not an option as the other 27 Member States would have informally only debated Brexit on that occasion The alternative would have been October or December 2016. But the magnitude of the Brexit earthquake risked being so great that the project could have been dropped altogether. In those first hours after the fateful referendum, whose results hardly anyone in the Brussels bubble had seriously contemplated, the general sense of panic and bewilderment was such that the EUGS, if postponed, risked being locked up in a drawer forever.

The HRVP felt that dropping the EUGS would have done a great injustice to the Union. As detailed above, the EUGS had been the outcome of almost 2 years of an EU-wide strategic reflection, a deliberation which had seen the active involvement of all the Member States and the broader foreign policy community. All the 28 Member States and EU institutions were satisfied with the result. As the HRVP put it to me on the evening of the 24th June: "The work is done". So why did the document have to be shelved? Isn't it precisely at such times of crisis that manifesting European unity, which is precisely what the EUGS advocates for the Union, becomes an act of political responsibility? True, in June 2016 the EUGS would not have received the attention that some felt it deserved by the European Council or by the media. But arguably believing that a long-term strategic document of such kind would have ever made the headlines or been subject to detailed deliberation by the European Council was naïve. In any case, it was not the point of the exercise.

As discussed in Chap. 2, the purpose of the EUGS was captured by its title "Shared Vision, Common Action". The first aim was precisely the process of strategic reflection which culminated in the Strategy, an extensive and intensive process that succeeded in achieving considerable discursive convergence among all players, an achievement that all the Member States openly acknowledged. The strategic reflection had succeeded in giving rise to a shared vision: the EUGS had to see the light of day.

The second aim was to spur what comes after a shared strategic reflection: namely common action. The EUGS had to be published in order to start the engines on the implementation. The EUGS could not simply be parked in view of Brexit, waiting for more propitious times. It had to be put into action precisely because the EU's predicament was so calamitous.

In retrospect, the HRVP's decision to proceed with the publication of the EUGS was wise. While one year on after the UK referendum, the Brexit fog is still thick—beyond the tautological "Brexit means Brexit"— quite a bit of common action spurred by the EUGS is already underway.

Notes

1. The December 2013 European Council Conclusions mentioned a report to be produced "in the course of 2015" (European Council 2013).
2. In an open letter by the European Council on Foreign Relations, 50 European personalities stated: *'With planes being shot down over Ukraine,*

the Middle East descending further into sectarianism, and tensions mounting in Asia, this is not a time for novices.' ECFR Open letter, 20 August 2014.
3. For reports of these meetings, and of the public outreach of the strategic reflection, see http://europa.eu/globalstrategy.
4. See http://europa.eu/globalstrategy.

REFERENCES

European Council. 2003. *Presidency Conclusions.* Thessaloniki, 19–20 June. http://data.consilium.europa.eu/doc/document/ST-11638-2003-INIT/en/pdf.

European Council. 2013. *Presidency Conclusions.* Brussels, 19–20 December. http://www.consilium.europa.eu/uedocs/cms_data/docs/pressdata/en/ec/140245.pdf.

European Council. 2015. *Presidency Conclusions.* Brussels, 25–26 June. http://consilium.europa.eu/en/meetings/european-council/2015/06/euco-conclusions.pdf.

European Parliament. 2016. *Report on the EU in a Changing Global Environment: A More Connected, Contested and Complex World.* 29 March. http://www.europarl.europa.eu/sides/getDoc.do?type=REPORT&reference=A8-2016-0069&language=EN.

EU High Representative. 2003. *A Secure Europe in a Better World. European Security Strategy.* December. https://www.consilium.europa.eu/uedocs/cmsUpload/68367.pdf.

Howorth, Jolyon. 2016. EU Global Strategy in a Changing World: Brussels' Approach to the Emerging Powers. *Contemporary Security Policy* 37 (3): 389–401. doi: 10.1080/13523260.2016.1238728.

Missiroli, Antonio, ed. 2016. *Towards an EU Global Strategy: Consulting the Experts.* Paris: EUISS. http://www.iss.europa.eu/uploads/media/EUGS_Expert_Opinions.pdf.

Mogherini, Federica. 2014. *Hearing at the European Parliament.* Brussels, 6 October. http://www.europarl.europa.eu/hearings-2014/en/schedule/06-10-2014/federica-mogherini.

Mogherini, Federica. 2015. *Speech at the Munich Security Conference.* Munich, 8 February. http://eeas.europa.eu/statements-eeas/2015/150208_01_en.htm.

Pew Research Center. 2016. *Europeans Face the World Divided.* Pew Survey, June. http://pewrsr.ch/1WIdvUf.

Waterfield, Bruno. 2016. EU Army Plans Kept Secret From Voters. *The Times.* 27 May. http://www.thetimes.co.uk/article/eu-army-plans-kept-secret-from-voters-3j3kg3zwj.

CHAPTER 4

What Is a Strategy?

The Journey from the ESS to the EUGS

In 2003, the European Union was full of confidence and hope. In 2003, we lived in an international liberal order in which the belief in an imminent *End of History* was widespread (Fukuyama 1992). We lived in a world in which US hegemony was still unchallenged and the broad conviction in Europe was that by "acting together, the European Union and the USA can be a formidable force for good in the world" (EUHR 2003: 20). We lived in a world in which many countries were knocking at the EU's door, and in which the EU as such was viewed as a model and source of inspiration by many across the globe.

The ESS was premised on the understanding of a Union as an island of peace and prosperity, whose mission in the world was to radiate outwards its internal achievements thus transforming others. In this respect, the EU would take special responsibility in its surrounding regions to the east and south. Through its expansion, the EU would consolidate peace and prosperity on the continent. Furthermore, by devising an enlargement-like policy, the EU would benignly spread its norms, rules and standards to what became known as the "neighbourhood". In other words, the EU would help others become more like itself, be it through enlargement or through what was to become the European Neighbourhood Policy (ENP). The international position of the Union in those years inspired a deep sense of self-confidence, which overran almost inadvertently into hubris: the very term "neighbourhood", a term

© The Author(s) 2017
N. Tocci, *Framing the EU Global Strategy*, Palgrave Studies in
European Union Politics, DOI 10.1007/978-3-319-55586-7_4

first coined by then Commission President Romano Prodi, much like the concept of a "ring of friends" in the ESS, and their largely uncontested use at the time including in the academic literature, speaks volumes of the Eurocentrism of those times.

The EU would leverage the desire of third countries to deepen relations with the Union to support their domestic transformation in line with European standards. At the time, this did not strike readers of the ESS as evidence of Euro-hubris. In 2003, there really was a long queue of countries wishing to become EU Member States beyond the central and eastern European soon-to-be members, beginning with the Western Balkans and Turkey, as well as countries that eventually entered the ENP. Turkey, in particular, was undergoing a silent revolution, in which democratisation and economic modernisation went hand in hand with the country's Europeanisation. Even in the case of Russia, while EU membership was never seriously considered either by the Union or by Russia itself, a common mantra in Brussels and Moscow in the 2000s spoke of a free-trade area spanning from Lisbon to Vladivostok (Spiegel Online 2010).

It is in this context that the 2003 ESS advocated "a ring of well-governed countries" to the EU's east and south, setting out the ambition, in retrospect the illusion, that the EU would achieve just that (EUHR 2003: 12). It would achieve this goal by completing enlargement, which was "making a reality of the vision of a united and peaceful continent" (EUHR 2003: 3). But while the EU was intent on "avoiding new dividing lines in Europe" (EUHR 2003: 13), enlargement could not continue forever. Whereas during the 1990s resistance to enlargement was marginal and confined—particularly to France—by 2003, the first inklings of what soon became an entrenched "enlargement fatigue" across the Union were beginning to surface. The EU was therefore determined to replicate the method, but not necessarily the finality of enlargement in order to create a ring of stable, democratic and prosperous neighbours. It would extend "the benefits of economic and political cooperation to our neighbours in the East" (EUHR 2003: 13), applying, *mutatis mutandis*, the conditionality, socialisation and technical harmonisation that underpinned the enlargement process (Kelley 2006). The seeds of what became the European Neighbourhood Policy were sown back then.

Beyond the immediate "neighbourhood", the EU would defend the international liberal order, preserving its underlying norms and multilateral nature. It would contribute to an "international order based on effective multilateralism" by "spreading good governance, supporting social and political reform, dealing with corruption and abuse of power, establishing the rule of law and protecting human rights" (EUHR 2003: 14). The ESS highlighted the need for a comprehensive approach to failed states and regional conflicts, which blended military and civilian instruments—thereafter known as the "comprehensive approach to conflicts and crises". It praised the role of and promised support for regional organisations, and it stated that for those who violate such norms "there is a price to be paid, including in the relationship with the European Union" (EUHR 2003: 16). Talking of prices to be paid, in its concluding section, the ESS called for "a strategic culture that fosters early, rapid, and when necessary, robust intervention" (EUHR 2003: 17). For a generation of policy-makers on whose minds the failure to intervene early in the Balkans was constant and vivid, rapid and robust intervention was not associated with the unleashing of chaos, violence and human rights abuses as it is today. It was rather synonymous to being a good international citizen: it constituted the recognition, by no means universal at the time, that other people's wars mattered to us too.

The confidence and optimism with which the EU was imbued at the time did not translate into an unrealistically benign view of the world. To the contrary, the ESS was clear-eyed about the threats facing Europe and the world: terrorism, weapons of mass destruction (WMD), regional conflicts, failed states and organised crime. Between the June and the December versions of the ESS, the articulation of threats became somewhat more detailed. The George W. Bush-centric emphasis on terrorism and WMD was complemented by a stronger emphasis on "older" security threats, including regional conflicts, failed states, organised crime and the interplay between the three, notably to the EU's east and south (Missiroli 2015).

The EU would address these threats and challenges working together with the USA. While not spelled out bluntly in the text, the driving rationale was that the EU would temper Washington's unilateral excesses, and the transatlantic partnership would preserve the multilateral system established after World War II. As put in the ESS, "no single country is able to tackle today's complex problems on its own" (EUHR 2003: 3). Interestingly in this respect, whereas in the June 2003 draft the ESS called for "pre-emptive engagement", in the December version the wording was changed to "preventive engagement", responding to Member States' concern that the original formulation was too reminiscent of the

2002 US National Security Strategy, the document which elevated the doctrine of US unilateralism to new heights (Missiroli 2015).

The political context of those months provides further insight into the explanation. The EU spoke about preventive engagement not only to provide a clever linguistic riposte to the US's doctrine of pre-emptive action. It was also because it was precisely what the EU was doing in practice at the time. The second half of 2003 was the time in which the seeds were sown for what eventually was to blossom into the E3 + 3 format to negotiate the Iranian nuclear file. In those months, France, Germany and the UK, having learned from their split over the war in Iraq, began working together to provide a common European approach to the threats emanating from the Middle East. Such an approach would not only constitute a distinctly European form of preventive engagement, but it would also need to be acceptable to and ideally valuable for the USA. Hence, the joint initiative in October by Foreign Ministers Dominique de Villepin, Joschka Fischer and Jack Straw vis-à-vis Iran no sooner had the news about Tehran's secret nuclear programme become public. By the fall of 2004, partly due to different political conditions within the EU and partly due to the Bush administration's greater openness towards European involvement in the Iranian nuclear file, HR Solana succeeded in joining his British, French and German peers. This initiative later crystallised into the E3/EU+3 format for negotiations with Iran coordinated by the HR: one of the greatest successes of EU foreign policy—or preventive engagement—to date.

Fast-forwarding to 2016, the EUGS on the one hand had to provide a degree of formal and substantive continuity with the ESS, but on the other had to respond to a fundamentally different geostrategic context and Union. The structure of the ESS was unpacked in two documents: the 2015 EU strategic assessment (see Annex A) of June 2015 and the June 2016 EU Global Strategy (see Annex B). In the strategic assessment of June 2015, the strategic reflection provided its "assessment of the global environment", which back in 2003 constituted the first section of the ESS—i.e. "the security environment". Like the ESS, the EUGS set out its "priorities", which in the ESS were defined as "strategic objectives". Unlike the ESS however, in the EUGS these priorities were articulated on the grounds of specified interests and principles, which the ESS did not delve into. As in the ESS, the EUGS concluded with the "so what for the EU?". But unlike the ESS and as explored in detail in Chap. 5, the EUGS was more precise than the ESS on the follow-up action necessary to implement the Strategy.

Far more complicated than structure was the relationship between the contents of the two texts. The optimism, confidence, idealism and, yes, hubris of the early 2000s could simply not be replicated in the EUGS in view of the more connected, contested and complex world of 2015–2016 (see Annex A). At the same time, the HRVP did not want to convey a political message of closure, defensiveness, defeatism or crude *realpolitik* to Europeans and the wider world. To the contrary, she wanted to convey an opposite message of openness and, yes, self-confidence. The EU would still have to stand united in engaging the wider world, and it would have to do so responsibly and in partnership with others. But it could not pretend that a ring of well-governed countries beyond its borders was within reach, nor that it had a magic wand to fix failed states, regional conflicts and terrorism within and beyond its borders. In other words, the pendulum had to move away from the outwards looking idealism of the early 2000s, without swinging all the way to the opposite end of defensive *realpolitik*. As discussed below, "principled pragmatism" was the notion that sought to square of the circle. The EU would pragmatically look at the world as it is, but it would approach the challenges and opportunities presented by it by living up to its own principles as well as by being more responsive to the views of others.

Similar to the ESS, the EUGS is organised in a fairly straightforward way. It begins by outlining the EU's interests and the principles that should guide its external action. It then sets out five main priorities for the EU and concludes by sketching the action areas the Union should focus on to achieve these. Yet behind every title, subtitle and sentence of the EUGS, conscious choices were made, often preceded by lengthy debates amongst a plurality of stakeholders. This chapter unpacks the content of the document itself, explaining the discussions and decisions made behind the scenes.

THE TITLE

Let's start from the beginning. The 2003 Strategy was called a European Security Strategy (ESS). Why was this tradition not followed in 2016? Why did HRVP Federica Mogherini not produce a revised ESS like her predecessor HR Javier Solana, but opted to produce an EU Global Strategy instead?

Right from the start, Federica Mogherini was determined to carry out this work as both High Representative of the Union for Foreign Affairs and Security and Security Policy and Vice-President of the Commission. From her first step as HRVP in the fall of 2014, she manifested her intention to wear fully her two hats. She said so clearly during her hearing at the European Parliament in October 2014 (Mogherini 2014). She signalled it by moving her main office across the other side of *Rondpoint Schuman* in Brussels, from the EEAS to the 11th floor of the European Commission's building, the *Berlaymont*. And she appointed as her first Head of Cabinet Stefano Manservisi, an old Commission hand. She immediately acted as VP by regularly participating in the weekly *College* meetings of Commissioners, by taking seriously her role as chair of the Commissioners' Group on External Action, and by often making joint statements and organising joint missions with her Commission peers, of which the visit to Iran with a large delegation of Commissioners a few months after the signature of the E3/EU + 3 nuclear deal in 2015 is the most salient example to date.

Wearing both HR and VP hats is not easy. Mastering the art of being an effective High Representative by taking the initiative and building consensus between Member States is a monumental task in its own right. Doing so while striving to be and being viewed also as a VP of the Commission is even more arduous. Notwithstanding the Lisbon Treaty's entry into force in 2009, old habits and institutional turf wars die hard. Some Commission officials were manifestly eager to engage in a strategic "whole of EU" exercise. These included not only those working in explicitly "external" services such as DG NEAR (responsible for enlargement and neighbourhood policies), but also several officials working in areas less commonly associated with foreign policy such as DG EAC (education and culture), R&I (research and innovation) or MOVE (mobility and transport). Others engaged less proactively. I am sure that some— never admitting this openly—have not fully metabolised the double-hatted role. Some still view the HRVP's position as an expression of the Member States rather than that of the Commission: it takes some persuading amongst Commission officials that the HRVP is also "their boss".

Notwithstanding these daily—at times petty—problems, Federica Mogherini persevered. This was not to mark a change from Ashton. It was partly due to nationality and political persuasion. As an Italian social democrat, born and raised on the bread and butter of European integration, Mogherini was instinctively drawn to her role in the European

Commission, as the guardian of the Treaties and the beating heart of the Community method of integration. It was also, and perhaps predominantly, due to the awareness that as an HRVP—as opposed to a national Minister of Foreign Affairs—the European Commission is where most of the EU's tools and instruments lie. The CFSP and CSDP are key elements of EU foreign policy. But while the fledging EEAS is precious and requires constant investment, and the CFSP/CSDP carries out important tasks, diplomacy and defence remain firmly under the grips of the Member States. In these areas, the HR's space for autonomous action is limited. By contrast, the competences falling under the remit of the Commission not only allow for greater autonomy, but also represent critical ingredients of twenty-first century foreign policy. Diplomacy and defence are crucial, but only alongside the use of trade, development, humanitarian assistance, education, research, transport, migration and mobility, amongst other policies and instruments. These competences could only be drawn upon by engaging fully the European Commission.

Here comes the reason for the title: the EU Global Strategy. At first glance, "global" can be interpreted geographically. Indeed, the ambition of the HRVP was to work on a geographically Global Strategy, which would reflect the EU's global presence and aspirations. While the EU's most pressing interests and responsibilities are clearly concentrated in its troubled surroundings to the east and south, and these regions are where the EU will make or break its reputation as a global player, developments closer to home are also shaped by dynamics further afield. This connectivity is one of the leitmotifs of the 2015 strategic assessment, which painted the picture of a more *connected*, contested and complex world (see Annex A). The Strategy therefore had to be "global" by openly acknowledging these global connections rather than resting comfortably on the EU's traditional mental maps such as the "neighbourhood". These maps are often institutional/discursive constructions which may partly shape but partly be disconnected from hard facts on the ground. One only needs to think of Da'esh to illustrate the point: formally Syria is a "neighbour" of the EU and is included in the framework of the ENP. Formally, Iraq is not: it belongs to a different region in the EU's institutional architecture. However, Da'esh straddles Syria and Iraq, as well as having presence, militants and sympathisers across North Africa and the Middle East, the Sahel and the Horn of Africa, the Balkans and the northern Caucasus, as well as in the EU itself. It would be surreal to develop a policy against Da'esh without factoring in these multiple global interconnections. The same logic applies to other world regions. A meaningful policy towards the eastern neighbours cannot be developed in isolation from policy towards Russia. At the same time, policies towards Russia are intimately connected to developments in other world regions, from Central Asia to the Middle East, and of course, the EU must bear in mind the growing interplay between Russia and China must be borne in mind. In other words, even a strategy that is primarily concerned with the EU's surrounding regions must be geographically "global".

But the most important reason why the HRVP did not want to produce a security strategy but rather a Global Strategy was functional. Functionally, the aim was to have a strategy that would be global by encompassing the full range of the EU's external action capacities. It is difficult, indeed impossible to think of a threat, challenge or opportunity that can be effectively tackled or seized through the use of a single policy or instrument. It is only a joined-up and tailor-made combination of specific instruments and policies which can deliver. This was indeed the main conclusion of the 2015 strategic assessment (see Annex A: 129–130). Such a joined-up approach required bringing together all those institutional players with external action competences: the European Council, the Council of Ministers in its Foreign Affairs, Development and informal Defence configurations, the Commission, the European Parliament and naturally the EEAS as well as the European Defence Agency. The EU Global Strategy was thus a strategy which the HRVP was determined to produce fulfilling all her roles, as High Representative, as Chair of the Foreign Affairs Council and as Vice-President of the European Commission, as well as Head of the EDA.

Initially, the working title for the EUGS was that of this book "A Stronger Europe in a Fragile World". The thinking behind this was to create a logical link with the 2003 ESS whose title was "A Secure Europe in a Better World", while acknowledging the fundamentally deteriorated geostrategic context. A "secure" Europe was no longer a given: the EU thus had to become "stronger" in order to be more secure. And it had to become stronger because the world was not proceeding towards the "better", but was displaying its multifaceted "fragilities". In the end, the HRVP opted against this working title for two reasons. First, and echoing the argument outlined above, the HRVP did not want to create a strict link to the ESS. The EUGS was not intended as a sequel to the ESS: it was a new product altogether first and foremost because of its more comprehensive—"global"—nature. Second, in the wake of Brexit, when the final touches on the EUGS were put, what mattered most was one single message: unity, that indispensable unity through which the Union and its Member States draw and project their strength. As explained in Chap. 2, political unity was one of the founding rationales for the EUGS. As we prepared to go to press on the 25th June, that plain and simple message became more vital than ever, hence the change of the title "*Shared* Vision, *Common* Action".

THE INTERESTS

The EU Global Strategy begins by setting out the EU's interests in foreign and security policy: security, prosperity, democracy and a rules-based global order (see Annex B: 131). The choice was not uncontested. Whereas the Treaties clearly set out the Union's values, explicitly stating that such values should inspire the EU's role in the world, nowhere in the Treaties are the EU's interests defined. The very word "interests" is somewhat of a dirty word in the EU vocabulary and has long been juxtaposed to values in the literature on European foreign policy too (Tocci 2008; Pace 2007). EU foreign policy has perennially juggled the uneasy relationship between interests and values. While discursively it has traditionally felt more at ease in "talking values", in practice it has generally opted for "doing interests", particularly if Member States' foreign policies are viewed as an integral element of EU foreign policy. The rich academic literature on "Normative Power Europe" has spilled much ink on the tense relationship between values and interests (Manners 2006; Hyde-Price 2006; Diez 2013). In the current environment of mounting security threats, had the traditional interests–values dichotomy been upheld in the EUGS, the scales would have likely tilted in favour of the former.

The HRVP and her team wanted to escape this bind. First, it is natural for the EU, as for any other international actor, to have interests in foreign policy. In fact, though the EU has never clearly articulated its interests as opposed to its values, it has often pursued silently the former while sidelining the latter, raising eyebrows and being accused of hypocrisy both by European scholars and by the recipients of European foreign policy abroad. And so why not uncover the cards by spelling out what the EU's underlying interests are? Should not values, rather than interests, be what the EU does without talking about them, while instead being more upfront and explicit about its interests? Second, by choosing only to spell out interests rather than values, the HRVP wanted to dispel the commonly held view of a dichotomy between the two. The "interests and values" debate has often become an "interests versus values" debate, in which in practice the values have ended up with the short straw. By avoiding presenting such a dichotomy in the Global Strategy, but rather by defining the EU's interests in a manner that would embed values, the aim was to point to the mutually constituting relationship between the two (Diez 2013).

Whereas in the academic literature, notably of social constructivist persuasion, the proposition of a mutually constituting relationship between interests and values is a no-brainer, it took some persuading amongst Member States and the Commission. Some felt that rather than taking values more seriously by embedding them in the definition of interests, we were in fact dismissing them altogether. They felt, in other words, that we were tilting towards a crude form of *realpolitik*. This was precisely the opposite of what the intention was. In the end, we pressed on with the case, with the HRVP repeatedly pointing to the tight inter-relationship between interests and values in her speeches and ultimately in the EUGS itself: "Our interests and values go hand in hand. We have an interest in promoting our values in the world. At the same time, our fundamental values are embedded in our interests" (see Annex B: 86). During the autumn of 2015, this relationship between values and interests was by far the most recurrent theme in discussions amongst my institutional interlocutors, including both the Member States and the European Commission.

In the end, what helped ease the debate was to disclose the actual content of these much-maligned interests. The EUGS states that the EU has four basic interests: security, prosperity, democracy and a rules-based global order. With the exception of a rules-based global order, which should be seen as the external condition for the fulfilment of the first three interests, the latter are first defined through their internal connotations. The EU has an interest in promoting the security and prosperity of its citizens and the vibrancy of its democracies. These internal interests, however, can only be fulfilled if accompanying external interests are pursued too.

European citizens will not be safe so long as there is violence, repression and instability in the EU's surrounding regions. Terrorism is the most obvious case in point. Likewise, in the twenty-first century in view of the greater connectivity and complexity of the international system, Europeans will not be prosperous without sustainable development and an open economic system worldwide. With most global growth expected to take place outside the EU in the coming decades, the EU's own development will increasingly hinge on its relationship with the outside world, be it through trade, investment, the digital economy or the movement of people. As Europe (and the USA) undergoes a wave of populist-inspired closure, this is a point which is far from uncontested, and had to be made clearly.

Finally, and perhaps most interestingly, the state of health of European democracies cannot be detached from the way Europeans engage with the outside world. When walls and fences are built to keep away refugees in search of protection in the EU, the moral blow to our internal democratic systems is incalculable. In other words, before preaching democracy to others, a first fundamental interest lies in securing the laws and values that underpin our own democratic systems. The way we conduct our external relations plays an important role in that respect. In this regard, the EUGS can be viewed as a "liberal" rather than as a "post-liberal" strategy (Juncos 2016: 12). But its liberal connotations are internal more than external. In other words, the EUGS stands firm on the affirmation of the EU's internal liberal values, which lie at the core of the European project. Its firmness on this point is all the more important given that those values are being questioned within, as evident with the rise of extreme right-wing populism across the continent. But this does not mean that the EU expects its internal liberal values to be adopted externally too. What it does mean is that the EU's internal democratic values, of which the respect for rule of law and international law is the key, should guide the Union's external policy. As explained below, the pragmatism with which the EU observes the world should not distract or detract from its commitment to the principles which underpin its foreign policy.

THE PRINCIPLES

By the late 2000s, with the onset of the global financial crisis, the rise of emerging powers and the resurgence of old ones, talk about US unipolarity started fading. In parallel with this global power shift from West to East, alternative visions of the world order started surfacing (Amsden 2001; Herd 2010; Zakaria 2008). The paradigmatic nature of this new constellation of power started being debated intensely. Many referred to an emerging multipolar system (Kupchan 2012; Mearsheimer 2001), in contrast with the bipolar system of the Cold War era and to the ephemeral but significant unipolar moment in the 1990s and early 2000s (Krauthammer 2003; Nye 2002). Others talked of non-polarity or inter-polarity, as alternative concepts to capture both the geographical power shift and the power diffusion beyond state boundaries (Haass 2008; Grevi 2009; Peterson et al. 2016). But irrespective of whether the future world would be multipolar, inter-polar or non-polar, by the 2010s the debate in Europe converged on the notion of multiple centres of authority within and beyond the West as a key feature of twenty-first century international politics.

This rapidly shifting global environment coupled with the global financial crisis began taking its toll on the EU's foreign policy ambitions. In a world in which the West would no longer be the unchallenged hegemon, the EU's own approach had to be reassessed. The working hypothesis could no longer be that of a world moving westwards towards liberal democratisation and free market modernisation, in which the USA and the EU would co-lead this westwards journey. Other directions of travel became eminently possible. Events within and at the borders of the EU shattered old European convictions further. The Eurozone crisis and the deep economic recession particularly in southern Europe, the rise of populist Euroscepticism, the implosion of the Middle East, Russia's assertiveness in the east, terrorist attacks in European cities and Brexit all triggered a deep self-questioning within the EU. Far from spreading its norms and values to the world, nationalists and populists, nativists and violent jihadists were spreading their ideas to the EU. The EUGS had to set out the principles that would reflect and react to this fundamentally transformed context within and beyond the Union. It spelled out four principles: engagement, responsibility, unity and partnership (see Annex B: 133–135).

In this dramatically deteriorated environment, the EUGS sought to resist the lure of retrenchment. In a Union faced with multiple crises and challenges, within and without, the temptation is that of burying heads in the sand and looking inwards. This could mean different things: stepping back from a global free-trade agenda, scaling back diplomatic activity, cutting development and defence budgets, and putting up walls and fences to keep migrants and refugees outside. Indeed, Member States have succumbed to many of these temptations, with Hungary's fences against refugees, German and French popular backlash against the Transatlantic Trade and Investment Partnership and the stark cuts to Member States' defence and development budgets during and after the onset of the global financial crisis being well-known examples. Pointing in the opposite direction, the EUGS argued that the EU must engage with the wider world. The greater connectivity of our times means that, for good or bad, the world will come to the EU even if the EU seeks to close itself off from the world. A friend put it to me using an analogy I found compelling and used in the EUGS: "The Union cannot pull up a drawbridge to ward off external threats. Retreat from the world only deprives us of the opportunities that a connected world presents" (Annex B: 134). This proposition may appear obvious to the foreign policy community, be it in official institutions, academia, think tanks, civil society or the media. But it is certainly not the knee-jerk reaction in other policy communities, including Heads of State and Government, who increasingly take key foreign policy decisions and were the ultimate recipients of the EUGS, hence the need to make the case for *engagement* in the Strategy.

This did not mean to say that any form of engagement would do. Engagement must be responsible. There are many interpretations of what such *responsibility* means but perhaps the most relevant is the call to act promptly but not rashly and single-mindedly, factoring in the harm that rash interventionism can cause. When, during the Christmas break in December 2015, I stumbled across David Campbell's (1993) book *Politics without Principle*, it struck me that this was precisely what we were attempting to do: a foreign policy that is responsible by not proceeding unabashed even when doing so supposedly in the name of values, but rather by listening to others without, however, falling in the trap of cultural relativism. Engagement had to be responsive, embedded in deep knowledge of the local context in which it is carried out. Engagement also had to be patient, dispelling illusions that quick fixes are readily available.

Responsible engagement also required *unity* within and *partnership* outside the EU. The argument made in the EUGS is that Member States acting unilaterally can hope to achieve precious little in such a complex world. When drafting the EUGS, I inserted a sentence, fearing that in the end it would not have survived the scrutiny particularly of the largest Member States: "As a Union of medium- to small-sized countries, we have a shared European interest in facing the world together". I was curious to see whether all Member States, including the largest ones, appreciated that in the twenty-first century world they were little more than small- to medium-sized countries, and therefore, European unity was an essential precondition for them to address their interests and wield influence in world affairs. I was pleasantly surprised that no one blinked and the sentence survived. After the Brexit vote, when we were making the final revisions to the EUGS on the 24th June, the HRVP elevated the principle of unity right at the top. Unfortunately, the majority of voters of one large Member State seemed to live in the illusion that going it alone in the 21st is instead a realistic option.

To the contrary, even the EU, with its 500-million citizens and economic might, can only achieve limited results by acting alone. The Union therefore had to refine its art of partnering, not limiting itself to states, international or regional organisations, but opening up much more to non-state actors too, including civil society and the private sector. In specific policy areas, such as cyber or peacebuilding, it is impossible to imagine meaningful EU impact without effective partnerships with the private sector and civil society respectively. In a twenty-first-century world, which is more connected, contested and complex, unity and partnership are of the essence.

These four principles—engagement, responsibility, unity and partnership—were captured in what I consider to be the overarching philosophy of the EUGS: principled pragmatism. The EUGS reads: "We will be guided by clear principles. These stem as much from a realistic assessment of the strategic environment as from an idealistic aspiration to advance a better world. In charting the way between the Scylla of isolationism and the Charybdis of rash interventionism, the EU will engage the world manifesting responsibility towards others and sensitivity to contingency" (Annex B: 133).

But what does principled pragmatism mean? The most commonly heard view is that principled pragmatism means that the EU should "act in accordance with universal values (liberal ones in this case), but then follow a pragmatic approach which denies the moral imperatives of those universal categories" (Juncos 2016: 2). But as correctly noted by Juncos herself, such an interpretation entails a contradiction in terms: "The EU needs to be either pragmatic or principled; it cannot have it both ways" (Juncos 2016: 2). In fact, this is not how principled pragmatism should be read. The correct interpretation of principled pragmatism is not that the EU should compromise on its principles as a result of pragmatic interest-based considerations.

The point is rather that of saying that the EU should remove its rose-tinted glasses and pragmatically look at the world as it is, and not as it would like to see it. The pragmatism comes in the diagnosis of the geopolitical predicament the EU finds itself in. It echoes a rediscovery of pragmatist philosophy that entails a rejection of universal truths, an emphasis on the practical consequences of acts, and a focus on local practices and dynamics (Juncos 2016: 5; Joseph 2016: 379). This means accepting different recipes to build resilient states and societies, supporting locally owned pathways to peace, working with regional organisations which may look very different from the EU, and championing the transformation of the post-World War II multilateral system so as to make it more representative, even if this means a relative loss of power for the EU itself. In doing so, however, the Union should not fall into the trap of cultural relativism: EU pragmatism should be principled. While different pathways, recipes and models are to be embraced, international law and its underlying norms should be the benchmark of what is acceptable for the EU and what is not.

Principled pragmatism is no panacea. Policy-makers will often find themselves at a crossroad, having to make difficult choices without the luxury of knowing the chain of events which their decisions will unleash. Seeking to be pragmatic while at the same time principled will not be easy. But principled pragmatism is not a contradiction in terms and offers an approach to navigate the everyday dilemmas foreign policy-makers face.

THE PRIORITIES OF THE EUGS

This leads to a discussion on the five main priorities of the EUGS: the security of our Union, the resilience of states and societies in surrounding regions, an integrated approach to conflicts and crises, cooperative regional orders and global governance fit for the twenty-first century.

The Security of the Union

Originally, the HRVP wanted to begin from the global level—the priority on global governance—and then work backwards to the security of the EU itself. But as the weeks went by and the perceived insecurity of the Union rose due to developments within and beyond our borders, the order was reversed. As the EUGS puts it: "The Global Strategy starts at home" (see Annex B: 135).

A critical mass of Member States was very keen on putting security and defence upfront in the EUGS and sending a clear message that this is the area where a wake-up call is most urgently needed. They were keen to press the accelerator on deeper cooperation, if not integration, on security and defence. This increased prioritisation of security arose naturally from the mounting security threats within and beyond the EU. It comes as no surprise that France, which has seen the highest rate of terrorist attacks in the EU in 2015–2016, strongly felt that "the house is burning" as one official emphatically put it to me. The string of terrorist attacks, notably in Paris and Brussels, and France's invocation of the Lisbon Treaty's article 42.7 calling for mutual assistance between Member States, meant that the EUGS could not simply treat security and defence as business as usual. The Common Security and Defence Policy could not be limited to responding to external crises or helping third countries build up their security and defence capacities. The EU was called on to make a contribution to the protection of Europe and Europeans themselves, as the general sense of insecurity amongst the public escalated over the months. This call was echoed by the security and defence community within and beyond the official institutions, which, having seen to their dismay a ESS being "diluted" into a broader EU Global Strategy, wanted to make sure their baby was not entirely stolen from them. They wanted to make sure the EUGS would have strong hooks on defence so as to be able to launch specific follow-up work on European security and defence after the publication of the EUGS. The Commission, traditionally reluctant to work on defence, was also on board. This was partly due to the personal views of Commission President Juncker on a European army. Also important was the broader evolution of the defence debate within a Commission that prides itself for being more "political" after the first election of its president through the *Spitzenkandidaten* procedure, which saw the European Council appoint a candidate indicated by the European Parliament (EP) group that won most votes in the 2014 EP elections.

At the same time, Europeans realised they had to wake up on security because of the growing awareness that the USA may not always and automatically come to the rescue in future. During Obama's first term, one of the major foreign policy initiatives had been the so-called pivot to Asia. The pivot essentially amounted to a gradual yet consistent redeployment of US troops and assets from Europe and the Middle East to Asia. After the announced pivot in 2009, Russia's intervention in Ukraine and the escalating violence in the Middle East diverted Washington's attention away from Asia. But would the pivot resume in future?

There is an undeniable, and indeed understandable, structural trend underway. The Cold War ended almost three decades ago. The USA is now gearing up to face its growing rivalry with China in the Pacific. Europe is far removed from this new geopolitical space of confrontation, even if it will be caught up in it were it to happen. In view of this, it is only natural for the USA to turn its defence gaze elsewhere. In other words, with the growing quest for hegemony in the Pacific reopening, American interest in European security will likely decrease over time. At the very least, the responsibility for European security, or as Americans, would say the defence "burden" in Europe had to be shared more fairly across the Atlantic. This is a message that the Obama administration had been sending increasingly loudly and clearly over the years, albeit always rather gracefully. One only need to think back at the message that former US Secretary of Defence Robert Gates sent on the eve of his resignation in 2011, calling upon European NATO allies to pay their dues on defence. But Europeans stuck their heads in the sand and pretended not hear. Some Europeans, notably in western Europe, may eventually embrace this shift in America's security gaze. Others, notably in eastern Europe, are deeply troubled by it. All Europeans are generally disoriented about what to do about this message. Only 4 months after the publication of the EUGS, with the election of Donald Trump to the US presidency, this is a message which Europeans can no longer ignore.

This, however, had to be reconciled with a set of voices pointing in a different direction. Some Member States, while keen on security and defence in general, wanted to ensure that in no way would the EUGS challenge NATO's supremacy on collective defence, nor would it question the national sovereignty of Member States on defence matters. There is no hiding of the fact that the Transatlantic Alliance looms large in European debates on security and defence. This is far from being a British-only issue: NATO is viewed as the main defence framework for most if not all its Members, 22 of which are EU Member States. Even those Member States that would like to see the EU stepping up its defence efforts are wary of doing so in a manner that would be, or would be seen to be, antagonising to or duplicating NATO. As those EU Member States which are also NATO allies tirelessly repeat, they only have "a single set of forces". Hence, the EU and NATO must work in synergy. In the current economic and security predicament in which Europeans are in, no one can afford costly duplications. Other Member States, notably some of the non-NATO countries, felt uneasy about a strong focus on NATO in the EUGS and wanted to make sure that their status and autonomy as neutral or in any case non-NATO members would be fully respected and reflected in the Strategy. Other Member States along with segments of the EEAS, the Commission, the European Parliament, as well as human rights organisations, cautioned against an excessive security focus in the EUGS. They felt that this would have made the EU appear as excessively securitised and defensive.

The EUGS sought to provide a coherent and compelling answer to different impulses: Europeans must take greater care of their own security, because of the dangerous geography they inhabit and because an external guarantor of European security cannot be taken for granted in future (see Annex B: 135–138). Yet to take security more seriously, the Member States, where the competences in this field lie, can no longer afford to act alone or in an uncoordinated manner. Individually, they do not have the defence budgets to protect their citizens. Collectively, with time and effort, they could. Taken together, Europeans spend sums equal to approximately 50% of the US defence budget. But they certainly do not possess 50% of American capabilities but rather a mere 15%. The fragmentation of that spending results in costly duplications and gaping holes when it comes to expensive defence equipment that no Member State alone can afford. Those European holes were woefully exposed in 2011 during the NATO intervention in Libya.

In other words, defence cooperation between Member States must become the norm, rather than the exception, if Europeans are to start taking their own security more seriously. This does not mean that the EU will establish an army in the foreseeable future or that the EU will replicate or replace NATO. The point is far more down to earth and, to use a term dear to the EUGS, pragmatic. Europeans need to start cooperating more systematically in security and defence matters to acquire, develop and maintain the capabilities needed to keep Europe safe. Whether these capabilities are then used in an EU, NATO or UN framework becomes a second-order question, which the EUGS does not concern itself with. Whatever the preferred institutional framework is, be it today or in future, it is still Europeans that have to become more capable to act in security and defence, as no one else will do it for them.

Related to this, the EUGS pushed the debate forward concerning the Common Security and Defence Policy. Since 1992, what eventually evolved into CSDP has been in principle concerned with the so-called Petersberg Tasks. At the time, the Petersberg Tasks were spelled out essentially to clarify that CSDP would not seek to duplicate NATO, reassuring the latter, and in particular the USA. Given that NATO's core business is the collective defence of its Allies, the EU would keep away from Europe and concentrate its efforts on low intensity crises beyond the EU's borders, notably in the neighbourhood and in Africa. To crisis response, a second key function of CSDP was added over time: the capacity building of the security apparatuses of EU partners, again to the EU's east and south. Through over a decade of CSDP practice, CSDP civilian and military capacity building missions have come to represent the bulk of what the EU does in this field. CSDP capacity building missions have been praised by outside observers as providing a key service which other security providers are less attuned to. But in the current geopolitical environment within the EU itself, the Union had to make a step forward: alongside external crisis response and capacity building, the protection of Europe had to be highlighted as the priority task for CSDP in the years ahead. The EUGS therefore added to the traditional tasks of the CSDP—crisis management and capacity building—a third one: the protection of Europe. This did not mean that the CSDP would start doing hard-core collective defence, an area which remains firmly in the hands of NATO. But it would mean that the EU should start concerning itself more with issues such as counterterrorism, hybrid threats, cyber security, and the protection of land, air and sea borders and critical infrastructure: all areas that lie at the nexus between internal and external security. This is the argument made in the EUGS, and later on taken up in the Implementation Plan on Security and Defence, to which all Member States subscribed.

The Resilience of States and Societies in Our Surrounding Regions

As suggested by the articulation of the EU's interests at the outset of the EUGS, the security of the Union hinges on peace and stability beyond its borders. This observation is not new. Already in the 2003 ESS, the EU set out to promote "a ring of well-governed countries" to the east and south as an integral element of its own security. The recipe back then was that of Europeanisation. By radiating its norms and values outwards, the EU would promote peaceful and well-governed countries beyond its borders. It would do so through the enlargement policy and through what was to become the ENP. Even when it came to countries such as Russia, particularly under Dmitry Medvedev's rule, the name of the game was that of Europeanisation. The four common spaces for cooperation between the EU and Russia, inscribed into the framework of the Partnership and Cooperation Agreement between the two, were informed by the general understanding that Russia would approximate EU laws and standards across different policy areas.

Today that world is gone. True, there are still countries that have opted for democratisation and modernisation through Europeanisation. The countries of the Western Balkans, to a (dramatically decreasing) extent Turkey, and a handful of countries in the ENP, would still like to move closer to EU norms and standards. The EUGS acknowledges this fact and recommits to these countries, which often feel abandoned by a Union that seems to have no wind left in its enlargement sails (see Annex B: 139–141). But beyond this limited number of countries, most neighbours to the east and south are not pleading to become more like the EU. In truth, this was the case also in the early 2000s. But the Union, buoyed by the enlargement success at the time, failed to see this. Today no one can hide the fact that towards all these countries the challenge is that of developing a "real" foreign policy and not just surrogate for enlargement: a foreign policy which would address state fragility, which would listen more than it preached, which would support more than it dictated.

The resilience of these countries is highlighted as a goal in the EUGS. The term "resilience" was chosen as a priority for two reasons. First because resilience is a term that speaks to two policy communities which the EUGS sought to bring together: the security community and the development community. Resilience often means different things to these two groups. I found fascinating for instance how some of my French interlocutors, who tended to view the EUGS exclusively through a security lens, translated resilience into *résistance*: a word with very obvious security connotations. This interpretation was far removed from that given by most human rights and development NGOs I engaged with, which emphasised instead the developmental, including psychological, dimensions of resilience. Differences notwithstanding, the resilience of states and societies in the EU's east and south was a goal that both policy communities shared and could converse about.

The second reason for choosing "resilience" is that it reflected the notion of principled pragmatism. As said above, the EU had to be pragmatic. It had to remove its rose-tinted lenses that depicted a world that simply wanted to look like the EU. Many countries to the EU's east and south have no such intention. At the same time, the EU could not simply abandon the transformational agenda in favour of a crude transactional one, in which even the most egregious violations of rights and law by states beyond the EU's borders would be ignored nonchalantly by the Union. Resilience sought to capture that middle way. As put by Wagner and Anholt (2016: 4), resilience provides "a middle ground between overambitious liberal peacebuilding and under-ambitious stability". The EUGS sees resilience as the ability to absorb, react and respond to shocks and crises. A resilient state is thus one that is able to survive change by changing itself: just like a resilient metal it bends but does not break. Hence, the EUGS claims that authoritarian states are not resilient in the long term. They may appear to be extremely stable, at times immobile. They may indeed remain so for years and decades. One only needs to think about regimes such as North Korea to realise that the long term may be very long indeed. But when a shock or crisis does occur, the brittleness of authoritarian states emerges in full force. Faced with shock, they tend to break altogether. The 2011 Arab uprisings are a testimony of that and should not be forgotten at times in which escalating violence and instability in the Middle East lures many in Europe to back unconditionally apparently stable, yet deeply fragile, authoritarian regimes in the region.

A resilient state and society therefore needs to be secure, but it also needs to be inclusive, well governed, developed, cohesive and sustainable. However, this does not mean that there is a single recipe to achieve such resilience, namely the implementation of the EU's *acquis communautaire*. The EU's *acquis* has served very well its Members, including those that entered the Union in 2004. In this respect, it is worth recalling that Poland and Ukraine shared similar economic standards when the Soviet Union collapsed. Clearly, Poland today is more resilient than Ukraine, whose weakness has invited Russian intervention. But while Europeanisation "works", the EUGS recognises that it is not the only way for a bright future. There is no-one-size-fits-all resilience: "there are many ways to build inclusive, prosperous and secure societies" (Annex B: 141).

The EU would therefore support different paths to build resilient states and societies and would do so in what it defines as its surrounding regions. The term neighbourhood was deliberately dropped. In fact, while the EUGS makes references to the ENP and on occasions refers to the EU's "neighbours", nowhere does it define its surrounding geography as the "neighbourhood". It rather speaks more broadly of "surrounding *regions*" (emphasis added). On the one hand, the EUGS wanted to signal that it viewed the resilience of states and societies as important not only in the countries falling within the scope of the enlargement policy and the ENP, but also beyond, stretching east into Central Asia and south into Central Africa (see Annex B: 139–143). On the other hand, the EUGS wanted to abandon the term "neighbourhood", which conveys a Eurocentric vision of a homogenous space beyond the EU's borders, a vision which is blatantly detached from realities on the ground. Not only are there huge differences between east and south. But the predicament and aspiration of each and every "neighbour" are to be accounted for in their own right.

An Integrated Approach to Conflicts and Crises

The third priority of the EUGS is an integrated approach to conflicts and crises in surrounding regions to the east and south (see Annex B: 143–146). One of the offspring of the 2003 ESS was what is commonly known as the "comprehensive approach". The most common interpretation of the comprehensive approach is the notion that the EU ought to approach conflicts and crises by blending all its policies, most importantly its security and development instruments. This traditional interpretation of the comprehensive approach remains relevant to this day. For years, policy-makers working on security and development have had an uneasy relationship, with the latter staunchly resisting the former's attempt to use development funds for security purposes. Over the course of the strategic reflection in 2015–2016, that debate reignited after a first agreement in 2015 to establish what became known as Capacity Building for Security and Development (CBSD). No sooner had the inked dried regarding the first sketchy agreement on CBSD, than old disagreements flared up again. The security policy community interpreted CBSD as the final green light by the Commission to use development funds to acquire the necessary kit and equipment to back up CSDP capacity building missions. The Commission rejected this interpretation arguing that EU development funds could not be used for defence purposes. At the time of writing, the tug of war goes on between Member States and the Commission on what CBSD actually is and what funds it should be able to draw from.

But the EUGS did not want to stop at instilling a new lease of life in the old comprehensive approach. It therefore used a different term—integrated approach—to signal what had to be added to it. Beyond the multidimensional approach blending security and development, the EUGS called for a multiphased approach along the whole conflict cycle, a multilevel approach focusing on the local, national, regional and global levels of conflict, and a multilateral approach by partnering with all the relevant regional and global actors in a given conflict configuration.

When highlighting the need to act at all stages of the conflict cycle, the EUGS emphasised the prevention and stabilisation phases of conflict. Conflict prevention is an area where the EU has already proven its more than occasional successes, be it in Montenegro, the Former Yugoslav Republic of Macedonia, Kosovo, Indonesia or elsewhere. The EUGS, recognising this fact, highlighted the need to further invest in prevention, notwithstanding the multiple crises which have already broken out around the Union. The EUGS also emphasised the stabilisation phase of conflict, that is after the crisis has exited its most acute violent phase but before it enters into long-term peacebuilding. As always, the choice was conditioned heavily by context, and particularly the need to pay attention to those areas of Iraq, Syria as well as Libya which had been liberated by the Islamic State, but which could easily relapse under Da'esh's control if abandoned to their own devices.

Also worth highlighting is the emphasis placed on the local and regional levels of such conflicts when discussing a multilevel approach to conflicts and crisis. The EUGS recognised that most conflicts, and particularly those to the EU's south, are marked by local, national, regional and global levels. It is the interaction of these four levels that makes such conflicts so intractable and protracted. It is only by acting at all such levels that the EU can hope to make a meaningful difference on the ground. So, whereas the ESS, informed by European passivity in the Balkans, mentioned the need for rapid and robust intervention at international level, the EUGS, influenced by the failure of such interventions in Afghanistan, Iraq and Libya, does not. This is not to say that the ESS believed in international military quick fixes and the EUGS does not. It rather means that in view of the different experiences which preceded the two exercises, the EUGS took a more sober view. It discusses what the EU can do at the international level—including through military means—to facilitate, mediate and support locally owned and regionally embedded agreements. Some would argue that this denoted a reduced level of military ambition in the EUGS compared to the ESS. As said, I believe that it rather reflected a recognition that the robust interventions that took place after 2003 did not produce sustainable results. Hence, different approaches, including to the way in which military instruments are deployed, had to be considered. It may well be that many of these conflicts will not be "solved" for many years. Cases such as Syria, Libya or Yemen most certainly fall in this category. Yet even in these cases, the EU must act patiently on the ground, aware of the intricacies of everyday local politics and regional dynamics, doing what it can in order to support locally owned peace (Richmond and Mitchell 2011). Rather than preparing for the crises of yesterday, the EUGS implicitly argued that it is worth learning from the past and prepare for crises of today and of tomorrow.

In view of the multiple levels of conflicts, the integrated approach also highlights the imperative of developing a multilateral approach to their resolution. The EU must develop agile and responsive ways of partnering with all the relevant actors in a given conflict configuration. This "partnering" does not necessarily mean that all such actors will be "partners" of the EU, but rather that the Union recognises that a particular conflict cannot be solved without working with them. Hence, the EU must and does "partner" with regional players such as Iran or Saudi Arabia and international ones like Russia when addressing the conflict in Syria. But this does not mean that such players will be EU partners in each and every international theatre. To the contrary, it factors in that in other situations these players may have different interests and goals, or may simply not be relevant at all.

Cooperative Regional Orders

While the first three priorities referred to a broad geography—the EU and its surrounding regions—they were not organised geographically but rather thematically: security, resilience and conflicts. I had strongly resisted the notion of a geographic organisation of the text, which would have risked making it uninteresting and quickly outdated. I also wanted to avoid falling into old mental maps: the neighbourhood, Africa, Asia, and the Transatlantic relationship. Given that in the strategic assessment (see Annex A: 104–107) we had made a big deal about the growing connectivity within and between these regions, we could not simply ignore this in the EUGS itself.

At the same time, a space had to be devoted in the strategy to specific countries and regions such as the USA, Russia or China. Academics would have probably preferred a strategy organised only conceptually and not geographically, but a complete absence of geography would have resulted in an abstract strategy in which policy-makers would have lost their bearings. To bring geography back but in a non-traditional way, I had originally thought of organising the fourth priority of the EUGS by looking at the four cardinal directions from the EU: a West that would have included North, Central and South America; an East from the Western Balkans and the Eastern neighbours through Russia and to China and East Asia; a south from North Africa and the Middle East down to sub-Saharan Africa, and a North comprising the Arctic. The idea was a bit too unconventional for my institutional interlocutors so I yielded. I remained firm though on the idea that our old mental maps had to be rejigged. In the end, we kept together the Americas in the Atlantic space, as well as the Middle East and Africa in a broader South, but we separated the European space from Asia, paying the price of an insufficient focus on the growing interconnections between the two across the Eurasian landmass (see Annex B: 146–151).

The dilemma was then that of finding an overall organising principle for this priority that would have otherwise been a rather tedious listing of goals for each country and region. We opted for the notion of cooperative regional orders as a goal the EU would promote across these macro regions. However, the wording had to be carefully calibrated.

On the one hand, several Member States were keen not to leave room for ambiguity: the EU would not embrace and support any form of regional order, particularly those coercively imposed upon others. Such forms of regional cooperation would not contribute to establishing "order" and should not be supported by the EU. What these Member States, notably from central and eastern Europe, had in mind was obviously Russia, and what they view as its attempt to coercively establish a Eurasian Union upon the eastern neighbours of the EU. There should be no mistake: the EUGS would not embrace President Putin's attempt to coerce a Eurasian Union upon its neighbours.

On the other hand, and particularly when it came to regions such as Africa, Latin America and Asia, the EUGS wanted to signal a clear departure from the past. When discussing regional organisations for instance, the Strategy discarded the notion that the EU is the only or even the best possible model to be followed by other regions. Regional organisations and regionalism are a far more important feature of international politics today than they were in the early 2000s (Telò 2014). Indeed, they occupy a more important place in the EUGS than the few passing references in the ESS. But the assumption in the EUGS is not that such organisations, if successful, would end up looking like the EU. The Strategy openly acknowledged that "Regional orders do not take a single form" and that "We will not strive to export our model, but rather seek reciprocal inspiration from different regional experiences" (Annex B: 146). In other words, in 2016, the EU was far more humble about the possibility of different futures and its own relative position in the wider world than it was in the early 2000s.

Global Governance

The same appreciation of a fundamentally different global environment and the EU's role in it emerged in the EUGS's approach to global governance (see Annex B: 151–155). The EU's commitment to the multilateral system centred around the UN has remained unscathed. However, far more than in 2003, in 2016 the Union realised that transformation rather than mere preservation was necessary if it was serious about safeguarding multilateralism. The global power shift and power diffusion in what the EU dubbed as a more complex world (Annex A: 111–115) called for a change of approach. Existing multilateral institutions must become more representative of the global power configuration if they are to retain their relevance. If "old" powers—foremost EU Member States—obstinately cling on to their excessive share of the pie within the UN Security Council and the International Financial Institutions, these organisations will progressively lose their global standing and be replaced by alternative institutions. The establishment of the Asian Infrastructure and Investment Bank (AIIB) in 2014 was a warning signal, to be replicated in other areas if the system remains unchanged. Hence, as put by the EUGS, "A commitment to global governance must translate in the determination to reform the UN, including the Security Council, and the International Financial Institutions (IFIs). Resisting change risks triggering the erosion of such institutions and the emergence of alternative groupings to the detriment of all EU Member States" (Annex B: 152). Member States could not agree to the details of such reform. Discussions in the context of the EUGS failed to move forward the debate between the largest Member States, particularly when it comes to the reform of the UNSC, on which they remain bitterly divided. All we could "agree" on is a need for reform and on what the broad principles of such reform might be. (I put "agree" in inverted commas, as it was an agreement empty of meaningful content, although it was probably better than ignoring this key question altogether.)

Beyond representation and reform, the EUGS's transformational approach emerged through the emphasis on the need to invest in global governance, notably to support the UN's peacekeeping and humanitarian functions; to implement global governance in the areas of sustainable development and climate; to deepen global governance through bilateral and plurilateral trade agreements and to develop global governance in areas such as cyber, energy, migration and emerging technologies. In short, the deep transformations underway within the international system need to be reflected in global governance mechanisms if these are to be fit for purpose. And to become so, the EU would need to become far more proactive and transformational.

From Vision to Action

The final chapter of the EUGS ties together all the threads and addresses the "so what" question for the EU itself (see Annex B: 155–161). Given its interests, principles and priorities, what must change in the means and ways in which the EU does foreign policy?

First, it is made clear that the EU should invest more and more cooperatively in security and defence. This first line of action responded principally but not exclusively to the priority of the Strategy concerned with building a more secure Union. The necessary defence capabilities are spelled out in some detail, as well as the mechanisms to engender deeper defence cooperation between Member States. Almost hidden in the text here is the idea that part of the follow-up work on the EUGS would have to concentrate on the implementation of this strand of work through a dedicated line of action. A defence follow-up was not flagged too visibly because a formal decision by the Council on the matter had not been taken yet, and Member States were sensitive about the EUGS explicitly committing them in a policy area which falls firmly under their competence. But as discussed in the next Chapter, defence was indeed the area in which the most immediate, tangible and ambitious follow-up to the EUGS took place.

Second, it is emphasised that if the EU is to promote tailor-made formulas to build resilient states and societies, promote locally owned agreements, support cooperative regional orders and engage in a reform of global governance, its foreign policy should become more reflexive and responsive. EU foreign policy must be centred on a more granular understanding of what actually happens on the ground, and this requires investing more and better in diplomacy, and in particular on the quality of the EU's representation abroad. The European External Action Service should not be viewed as a 29th Ministry of Foreign Affairs in the EU. It should rather offer Member States a service which their national diplomacies cannot provide. To do so, the EEAS, as a unique yet still fledgling institution in the making, should feature the best and the brightest from 28 national diplomatic services plus the European Commission, blended into a European whole. Were it to achieve such a standard by bringing together a plurality of national cultures and experiences, the EEAS would not simply represent an *unicum* in Europe, but in the world as well. Achieving this would be far cheaper than building expensive military capacities, while very expensive if it went wrong.

Being more responsive also requires being able to use funds, and particularly the significant development funds at the EU's disposal, in a manner that is more political and flexible. In 2015, the EU's Foreign Policy Instrument commissioned a survey on the way in which the EU is perceived in the world (FPI 2015: 17). I was struck by the fact that development is one of the areas in which the EU is least visible, less than in diplomacy which remains a domain still largely controlled by the Member States. If the EU—including Member States—is by far the largest development actor worldwide, yet this is hardly visible to the rest of the world, then a serious rethink of development policy is necessary. EU funds should be able to act and react more rapidly and flexibly to the outbreak of crises and to unforeseen shocks. More broadly, development policy should become better equipped for a world that has become predictably unpredictable as put by the EUGS (see Annex B: 157). The Sustainable Development Goals agreed in 2015 at the UN, which for the first time openly acknowledged that areas such as conflict, governance, security and climate fall under the remit of development policy, should help the development community transition towards a more political role in world affairs. The EUGS wanted to capitalise on this opening and spur it forward.

Responsiveness is also critical when it comes to diplomacy. In principle, the EU has the unique advantage of being able to galvanise the energy and assets of 28 national diplomacies alongside the European External Action Service, which weaves their work together. In principle, alongside the HRVP, there are 28 ministers of foreign affairs, 28 development ministers and 28 defence ministers to be mobilised in the pursuit of shared interests and goals. The EUGS noted that, in practice, rather than multiplying exponentially the assets available, the sheer number of actors involved and the need for consensus in foreign policy decision making within the Council have reduced the capacity for rapid and responsive EU diplomatic action and reaction.

The large Member States, often feeling straight-jacketed by this set-up, increasingly operate in small groups outside the EU Treaties. The Normandy group, including France and Germany, set-up to deal with the crisis in Ukraine, is perhaps the best example of this trend. Yet not all small groups follow the same model. A very different model is that of the E3/EU + 3 that negotiated the nuclear agreement with Iran, perhaps the greatest success of EU foreign policy to date. Unlike the Normandy set-up, the E3/EU + 3 includes not only three Member States—France, Germany and the UK—but also the High Representative, alongside the USA, Russia and China. In the 2004, Javier Solana, then HR, had skilfully made his way into the format; Catherine Ashton kept the negotiation alive during the dark days of Mahmud Ahmedinejad presidency in Iran; and Federica Mogherini shepherded the group to a breakthrough when conditions were ripe under Presidents Obama and Rouhani in 2015. The value of including the EU—through the HR—into the format cannot be underestimated, both from an internal European perspective, and from the perspective of the external problem to be solved. This does not mean that the HR must necessarily be physically present in each and every contact group. But it does mean that in order to be effective and be viewed as legitimate, all Member States must somehow feel that smaller groups act in their interests. Therefore, a broader EU framework within which contact groups are embedded and ideally a role for the EEAS should be in place.

In other words, rather than fight back against the existence of contact groups—an undeniable reality of European foreign policy—the EUGS set out to embrace them conditionally and regulate them. Contact groups could help the EU develop a diplomatic role that is nimbler and more responsive. But contact groups have to be governed by criteria that ensure rapidity and flexibility do not come at the expense of the sovereign equality of Member States. The EUGS set out what such criteria may be. Painstaking negotiations took place on this point between larger Member States wanting to retain greater freedom of manoeuvre and smaller Member States that feared being dominated by an EU *directoire* of two or three big Member States. This was the very last knot to be untied on the eve of the 25th of June, when all other issues, from Russia to migration and defence, had been resolved. Towards the end of that day, I feared we would have had to drop the paragraph altogether, which would have been a shame as it is one of the most innovative points of the entire document. In the end, we reached an agreement and the paragraph on contact groups in the last chapter of the EUGS survived.

Finally, the EUGS, much like the strategic assessment, makes the case for a more joined-up Union. As explained at the outset of this chapter, this was supposed to be a Global Strategy that brought together the different actors, instruments and policies that collectively make up European foreign policy. But in order to make up a coherent whole, these different components have to be joined-up. The Strategy indicates some of the areas in which the joining up is most urgently needed. In particular, it highlights the need for more interaction, coordination and cooperation along the internal–external nexus—between actors and institutions dealing with the internal and external dimensions of the same or similar policy areas. Migration, in particular, deserves special mention in this respect. In reference to the EUGS, some Member States from the east were sceptical about making references to the internal dimensions of migration, notably asylum. Yet for a Strategy that made the internal–external nexus the silver thread running across the document, neglecting the internal dimension of the policy area—migration—where the internal–external nexus is most evident would have been paradoxical at best. By covering only the external dimension of migration, the Strategy would have given the impression that the EU's approach to migration is exclusively centred on keeping migrants outside EU borders. While, unfortunately, this is close to practice, other Member States and the HRVP herself did not want to give credence to such an approach in the EUGS. The internal–external nexus lies at the heart of the EUGS, and migration is perhaps the most poignant case in point. The document could not have ended without emphasising precisely this point.

The EUGS concludes with a paragraph on follow-up (see Annex B: 161). As detailed in the next chapter, the EUGS had to respond to the chorus of voices from Member States and EU institutions that had called for an "actionable" document early on during the process of strategic reflection. Hence, while the EUGS could not enter into these details, it had to lead the way towards implementation. The EUGS, as the title itself suggests, should be not only about forging a "shared vision" but also about pointing the way towards "common action". This meant indicating that the EUGS would be followed by specific new and revised sectoral strategies and plans. It also meant that some sort of review mechanism had to be established, so as to track the implementation of the EUGS and determine whether and when a revision of the Strategy was necessary. Finally, the EUGS indicated that it should not end up as another one off like the ESS. It refrained from spelling out a precise number of years before a new strategy would be developed. The EU is not a state, and as recounted in this book, the complexity of the process to produce a document like this is such that turning this into a rigid exercise to be carried out every 5 years, for example, would be neither feasible nor necessary. But in such fast-changing times, neither should an exercise like this be embarked upon after 13 years as was the case after the 2003 ESS. The time for a new strategy should be determined by events and political mood, rather than by the calendar.

REFERENCES

Amsden, Alice H. 2001. *The Rise of the "Rest". Challenges to the West from Late-Industrializing Economies*. Oxford: Oxford University Press.

Campbell, David. 1993. *Politics Without Principle: Sovereignty, Ethics, and the Narratives of the Gulf War*. Boulder: Lynne Rienner.

Diez, Thomas. 2013. Normative Power as Hegemony. *Cooperation and Conflict* 48 (2): 194–210. doi: 10.1177/0010836713485387.

EU High Representative. 2003. *A Secure Europe in a Better World. European Security Strategy*. December. https://www.consilium.europa.eu/uedocs/cmsUpload/78367.pdf.

FPI/European Commission Service for Foreign Policy Instruments. 2015. *Analysis of the Perception of the EU and EU's Policies Abroad: Executive Summary*. 7 December. http://ec.europa.eu/dgs/fpi/showcases/eu_perceptions_study_en.htm.

Fukuyama, Francis. 1992. *The End of History and the Last Man*. New York: Free Press.

Grevi, Giovanni. 2009. *The Interpolar World. A New Scenario*. EUISS Occasional Paper No. 79. Paris: EUISS. http://www.iss.europa.eu/uploads/media/op79.pdf.

Haass, Richard N. 2008. The Age of Nonpolarity: What will Follow U.S. Dominance. *Foreign Affairs* 87 (3): 44–56.

Herd, Graeme P. 2010. *Great Powers and Strategic Stability in the 21st Century: Competing Visions of World Order*. London: Routledge.

Hyde-Price, Adrian. 2006. 'Normative' Power Europe: A Realist Critique. *Journal of European Public Policy* 13 (2): 217–234. doi: 10.1080/13501760500451634.

Joseph, Jonathan. 2016. Governing Through Failure and Denial: The New Resilience Agenda. *Millennium: Journal of International Studies* 44 (3): 370–390. doi: 10.1177/0305829816638166.

Juncos, Ana E. 2016. Resilience as the New EU Foreign Policy Paradigm: A Pragmatist Turn? *European Security* 26 (1): 1–18. doi: 10.1080/09662839.2016.1247809.

Kelley, Judith. 2006. New Wine in Old Wineskins: Promoting Political Reforms Through the New European Neighbourhood Policy. *Journal of Common Market Studies* 44 (1): 29–55. doi: 10.1111/j.1468-5965.2006.00613.x.

Krauthammer, Charles. 2003. The Unipolar Moment Revisited. *The National Interest* 70: 5–17.

Kupchan, Charles A. 2012. *No One's World: The West, the Rising Rest, and the Coming Global Turn.* NewYork: Oxford University Press.

Manners, Ian. 2006. Normative Power Europe Reconsidered: Beyond the Crossroads. *Journal of European Public Policy* 13 (2): 182–199. doi: 10.1080/13501760500451600.

Mearsheimer, John J. 2001. *The Tragedy of Great Powers.* New York: Norton.

Missiroli, Antonio, ed. 2015. *Towards an EU Global Strategy: Background, Process, References.* Paris: EUISS.http://www.iss.europa.eu/uploads/media/Towards_an_EU_Global_Strategy.pdf.

Mogherini, Federica. 2014. *Hearing at the European Parliament.* Brussels, 6 October. http://www.europarl.europa.eu/hearings-2014/en/schedule/06-10-2014/federica-mogherini.

Nye, Joseph S. 2002. *The Paradox of American Power.* Oxford: Oxford University Press.

Pace, Michelle. 2007. Norm Shifting From EMP to ENP: The EU as a Norm Entrepreneur in the South? *Cambridge Review of International Affairs* 20 (4): 659–675. doi: 10.1080/09557570701680704.

Peterson, John, Riccardo Alcaro, and Nathalie Tocci. 2016. Multipolarity, Multilateralism and Leadership: TheRetreat of the West? In: *The West and the Global Power Shift*, ed. John Peterson, Riccardo Alcaro, and Ettore Greco, Transatlantic Relations and Global Governance, 43–73. New York, Palgrave Macmillan.

Richmond, Oliver, and Audra Mitchell, eds. 2011. *Hybrid Forms of Peace: From Everyday Agency to Post-Liberalism.* London: Palgrave Macmillan.

Spiegel Online. 2010. 'From Lisbon to Vladivostok': Putin Envisions a Russia-EU Free Trade Zone. *Spiegel Online*, 25 November. http://www.spiegel.de/international/europe/from-lisbon-to-vladivostok-putin-envisions-a-russia-eu-free-trade-zone-a-731109.html.

Telò, Mario (ed.). 2014. *European Union and New Regionalism.* London: Routledge.

Tocci, Nathalie. 2008. Profiling Normative Foreign Policy: The European Union and its Global Partners. In *Who is a Normative Foreign Policy Actor? The European Union and its Global Partners*, ed. Nathalie Tocci, 1–23. Brussels: CEPS. https://www.ceps.eu/node/1490.

Wagner, Wolfgang, and Rosanne Anholt. 2016. Resilience as the EU Global Strategy's New Leitmotif: Pragmatic, Problematic or Promising? *Contemporary Security Policy* 37 (3): 414–430. doi: 10.1080/13523260.2016.1228034.

Zakaria, Fareed. 2008. *The Post-American World*. New York: W.W. Norton.

CHAPTER 5

What Next After a Strategy?

THE EUROPEAN SECURITY STRATEGY AS A STRATEGIC CONCEPT

The European Security Strategy (ESS), in just over 4000 words, was never meant to be an "actionable" document. In its final chapter on policy implications, the ESS did point towards some strands of action, calling for "developing operations involving both military and civilian capabilities" and for "better coordination between external action and Justice and Home Affairs policies" (EUHR 2003: 17–19). More broadly, the ESS was associated with and partly fed a particularly dynamic phase of EU foreign policy. The European Neighbourhood Policy, the "comprehensive approach to conflicts and crises", and the establishment of the European Defence Agency are all in some ways daughters of the ESS. But the ESS never had an explicit implementation phase as its aftermath. Interestingly, the European Council meeting in December 2003, which adopted the ESS, had tasked HR Solana "to present, as appropriate, concrete proposals for the implementation of the European Security Strategy" (European Council 2003: para 86). The HR, however, ultimately decided that the ESS should remain a document outlining a general strategic narrative, rather than giving rise to specific and detailed action points. The ESS had done its job in bringing the EU together. In those days, there was no shortage of proposals for action. Changing direction and gear was not necessary. The 2008 Implementation Report was far more precise in this respect, specifying the role of the European Defence Agency, the Battlegroups and civilian response teams, as well as

© The Author(s) 2017
N. Tocci, *Framing the EU Global Strategy*, Palgrave Studies
in European Union Politics, DOI 10.1007/978-3-319-55586-7_5

opening the way to a host of sectoral strategies in areas such as counter-terrorism, non-proliferation, cyber security and maritime security.

The EUGS avoided the Implementation Report's shopping list approach to follow-up action and rather discussed policy implications by picking up similar themes to those of the ESS. The ESS spoke of a more "active", "coherent" and "capable" EU. The EUGS called for a more "responsive", "joined-up" and "capable" Union. The similarity between these policy/institutional themes denotes both a degree of continuity between the ESS and the EUGS, and a sober reminder of the unfinished work 13 years after the first Strategy was produced. However, in the ESS, these policy implications were only briefly sketched in a final page of the document. In fact, the ESS was only partially a strategy. It provided an overall vision, a sound analysis and a well-crafted set of overarching goals. But it said little about the means to achieve them, apart from a set of general indications. As defined by its main holder, the ESS was more a strategic concept than a strategy proper.[1]

By contrast, in the EUGS, these policy implications were elaborated at some length. The EUGS explained what kind of actions were necessary to make the EU more credible in security and defence, more responsive in the use of its financial instruments and in the organisation of its diplomacy, and more joined-up in areas that straddle the internal–external policy nexus such as migration, sustainable development or counterterrorism. Delving into some of these details—always within the parameters of a strategy, not an action plan—was essential in opening the way to the implementation of the EUGS, which for HRVP Mogherini, unlike her predecessor HR Solana, was essential.

In short, unlike the 2003 ESS, which outlined the goals but said little about the means to achieve them, the EUGS aimed at relating means to ends. It sought to address two questions: both the "what" and the "how". It did so in response to the calls for a new strategy to be "actionable" made by the Member States at the outset of the strategic reflection in early 2015. As explained in Chap. 2, the EU's predicament in 2015–16 was dramatically different than at the time of the 2003 ESS. Whereas back then, the principal demand was to forge a shared narrative that would capture the "European way" as already practiced through the EU's external action, in 2015–16 that action was generally deemed as insufficient or inadequate given the proliferating crises within and beyond the Union. The EUGS therefore had to both present a shared vision and point towards common action. Ultimately, the success or failure of the EUGS will be assessed against both these benchmarks.

This Chapter discusses the follow-up to the EUGS, in the first months after its publication. It does so by analysing the early performance of the EUGS against these two benchmarks: how was the shared vision received by the Member States, EU institutions, external players and the wider foreign policy community?; and what were the first steps towards common action stemming from the EUGS and how can these be assessed?

LAUNCHING THE EU GLOBAL STRATEGY

As discussed in Chap. 3, HRVP Mogherini decided to publish the EUGS notwithstanding the decision of most British voters to opt for Brexit. The HRVP's decision took many by surprise. A few, particularly think tankers from UK-based institutions, criticised the move, arguing that it signalled—yet again—the EU's other-worldliness, that the EUGS would simply be drowned in the tsunami of Brexit, or that there was something fundamentally wrong with the Strategy if it did not require a major rewrite after the UK referendum (Maçães 2016). Most others I spoke with, both from official institutions and beyond, applauded the move, arguing that it would provide a badly needed message about the EU's ability to stand united in such times of existential crisis.

So how was the EUGS received? Naturally, its publication was to an extent overshadowed by Brexit. The Strategy did not feature on the main evening news across the Member States, nor did it trigger a lengthy debate by Heads of State and Government at the European Council meeting held on 28 June 2016. The HRVP presented the EUGS at that meeting, but the session lasted not more than 30 min and the President of the European Council Donald Tusk chose not to open a discussion on the topic. In those early days following the Brexit trauma, the top leaders had bigger fish to fry.

But it is worth asking what would have happened had the UK referendum resulted in a Remain vote. Arguably, the reception of the EUGS would have been much the same. For, a subject such as this simply does not make it into breaking news and is not thoroughly examined by what has become the EU's short-term crisis management body *par excellence*: the European Council.

In the days and weeks after its release, the EUGS did feature in articles and op-eds in major media outlets, including the Financial Times, El Pais, Repubblica, Politico, Spiegel, Der Standard, Project Syndicate and To Vima, to mention a few. Think tanks were immediately busy dissecting the Strategy, and already by the autumn of 2016, two academic journals had published special issues on the subject (Contemporary Security Policy 2016; The International Spectator 2016). To the best of my knowledge, during the summer and autumn of 2016, dedicated conferences on the EUGS were organised both within and outside the EU, including Adelaide, Alpbach, Beijing, Belgrade, Berlin, Brussels, Canberra, The Hague, London, Melbourne, Paris, Prague, Rome, San Sebastian, Sydney, Tel Aviv, Trento, Turin, Vienna, Warsaw and Washington. Breaking news it was not, but it would be unfair to say that the EUGS passed completely under the public radar screen.

On content, views were generally positive. Some questioned the notion of "resilience" (Ülgen 2016; Biscop 2016; Wagner and Anholt 2016), while others problematised the bumper sticker of "principled pragmatism" (Juncos 2016). But with a few rare exceptions (Bendiek 2016; Smith 2016; Maull 2016), in the dozens of think tank pieces and academic articles I came across since June 2016, the general assessment was broadly positive. The shared vision the EU put forth through its Global Strategy was considered as coherent and compelling, striking the balance between realism and idealism, between ambition and reality, between engagement and protection, between doctrine and practice. After only a few months of the release of the Strategy, terms such as "resilience", "integrated approach", "joined-up EU", "strategic autonomy" and "principled pragmatism" were becoming staples of the EU foreign policy diet, within both academia and policy circles.

The recurrent, and in my view, correct note of caution in many articles and opinions regarded less the shared vision, but rather the common action (Techau 2016; Dijkstra 2016). Would the EU, in the sorry state of crisis, fragmentation and possible disintegration it is in, be able to translate its new shared vision into common action? Even though the EUGS was generally considered as realistic (Colemont 2016), was it realistic enough?

The big challenge indeed was, and is, the implementation of the EUGS.

THE IMPLEMENTATION OF THE EUGS

That implementation would be the biggest challenge was crystal clear to the HRVP from the very start. Several diplomats were consumed by the need to have some form of formal Council endorsement of the

EUGS following its publication. The European Council had only "welcomed the presentation" of the EUGS, a step above a "taking note of", and a step below a flat "welcoming" or "endorsement" of the EUGS in Euro-speak. The reason why the European Council did not squarely welcome the EUGS had to do with procedure, not with content. Although all the Member States had subscribed to every word in the Strategy, as discussed in Chap. 3, the text was officially circulated to the Member States only on 25 June, 2 days after the Brexit vote and 3 days ahead of the European Council. This gave Member States insufficient time to go through their national procedures for an approval, which in a few cases included parliamentary scrutiny. By October 2016, all but one Member State would have happily welcomed if not endorsed the Strategy. The one Member State that held back did so not because of reservations about the EUGS, but because of the linkage to another policy dossier largely unrelated to the EUGS.

Had the HRVP picked up that fight, she probably would have achieved a more formal endorsement by the Council, with the 27 Member States standing by her side. But the truth was that she was not too concerned by the issue. To her, what mattered most was concrete implementation. As far as she was concerned, the EUGS was out, the reception of it had been broadly positive, and virtually all her peers had congratulated her on her work in championing the EUGS as their shared vision. The shared vision, in other words, was there. Rather than picking a fight over the semantics of the Council conclusions' reference to the EUGS, the task was to move swiftly onto the common action.

Over the summer of 2016, the EEAS began working on a roadmap for the EUGS's implementation, listing the deliverables to be achieved by June 2017, when a first Implementation Report would be published to track the state of play in year one. The Roadmap featured a long shopping list of items, including a few big new initiatives, already planned initiatives which would need to be made EUGS-compliant, and several other existing policies or sectoral strategies, which had to be revised in order to bring them in line with the EUGS.

The roadmap was circulated to the Member States in September 2016 and formed the basis for the Foreign Affairs Council conclusions in October that year. Those Conclusions skipped the tricky Shakespearean choice of to welcome or not to welcome the EUGS, and jumped straight to the action, highlighting that the "this strategy [the EUGS] will guide the EU's external action for the years to come. The Member States are fully committed to its effective and prompt implementation jointly with the High Representative and the Commission" (Council of the EU 2016a).

The HRVP had always been adamant about the fact that the EUGS would need to be implemented in all policy spheres. This had been a refrain both during the strategic reflection and in the aftermath of the EUGS's publication. The need to make that call, time and time again, was closely linked to the very origins of the EUGS. The EUGS differed from its predecessor, the ESS, by being a "post-Lisbon Treaty" Strategy: a Strategy that addressed security and defence alongside a much broader array of EU external action instruments. As a functionally "global" Strategy, it left some unhappy and others half-committed.

Initially, the security and defence community felt their baby was being torn away from them. They only reconciled themselves gradually with the EUGS as they came to appreciate that it did take security and defence seriously rather than diluting them in a wider EU external action soup. Other policy communities within the remit of the European Commission—development, humanitarian assistance, neighbourhood and enlargement, trade, climate, energy, migration, mobility, education and research among others—also in the early days struggled to commit fully to the EUGS, preferring to sit comfortably within their policy silo rather than being viewed holistically within the remit of the Union's foreign policy. It took time to persuade both the initially unhappy defence community and the initially half-committed others that the EUGS was their responsibility. The same approach had to be followed through in the implementation phase.

Following the publication of the EUGS, the challenge was therefore twofold. The HRVP had to signal that in the implementation phase, security and defence would occupy a special place, but it would not be the only dimension of implementation. She did not want to give the impression that the previous 2 years of strategic reflection had been an unnecessary distraction, while in fact all that mattered was security and defence, with the rest being platitudes. The security and defence community had immediately started warming up its engines, feeling that their exclusive moment of glory had finally come. Their moment had come, but it was not their moment alone. The security and defence engines could start, alongside the implementation of other dimensions of the EUGS. This was particularly important to several Member States, notably the neutral Member States, that have traditionally felt more comfortable with the civilian than military dimensions of EU foreign policy. At the same time, the HRVP had to use fully her Vice-President's hat to ensure that through the complex and at times obscure procedures of the European Commission, the Commission-related priorities in the EUGS would feature in the Commission's work programme and therefore affect how resources are allocated and used by Commission services.

The October 2016 meeting of the Foreign Affairs Council adopted this broader approach to the EUGS's implementation. For the first year of implementation, it prioritised initiatives on resilience, on an integrated approach to conflicts and crises and on more joining-up of the EU's actions along the internal–external policy nexus in areas such as migration, hybrid threats and counterterrorism, public diplomacy, as well as security and defence. By the end of that month, the initiative on resilience was inserted into the Commission's work programme for 2017. The logic driving the selection of issues was a bit haphazard. The Council neither opted for a selection of the five goals of the EUGS—the security of the Union, resilience, the integrated approach to conflicts and crises, cooperative regional orders and global governance—nor of the three action points at the end of the Strategy—a more credible, responsive and joined-up Union. It rather mixed ends and means, selecting two of the former—resilience and the integrated approach—and two of the latter—a credible Union in security and defence, and a joined-up Union along the internal–external nexus. But to be fair, these were the issues that resonated most in both official and broader public debates. The Council added to these a work strand on public diplomacy, appreciating the effort made during the strategic reflection to reach out to the broader public. The Council rightly argued that public diplomacy should not stop with the publication of the EUGS. To the contrary, the launch of the Strategy should lead to a further boost of EU public diplomacy efforts, to which the Member States would have to be closely associated with.

TOWARDS A EUROPEAN SECURITY AND DEFENCE UNION?

Notwithstanding the effort to implement the entire Strategy, an approach dear to the HRVP and to several Member States, security and defence has been the area with the strongest wind in its sails since the publication of the EUGS. Why has this been the case and in what direction has this tailwind blown the Union?

Growing Insecurity

The broadest reason underpinning the push on European security and defence, predating the publication of the EUGS but becoming even more compelling thereafter, is the growing sense of insecurity within the Union. The gruesome sequence of terrorist attacks in the summer of 2016, or the Russian military build-up in the north, highlights this all too well. Indeed, opinion polls carried out in the summer of 2016 clearly pointed to the fact that security had become the number one concern for most European citizens (Pew Research Center 2016). The causes of insecurity differ widely between the Member States, with western and southern Europe fearing terrorism, while central, eastern and northern Europe are increasingly anxious about Russia's assertiveness. But causes aside, Europeans agree that security is their single greatest worry.

United Over Defence?

It is almost a euphemism to say that the EU is in crisis. Indeed crises there are plenty within and outside the European Union. Yet amidst the fray, and partly because of it, security and defence has emerged as the area in which Europeans stand more united. This represents a remarkable twist of history. Traditionally, foreign policy in general, and security and defence in particular, were the most divisive and controversial dimensions of the European project. As an area in which national interests are strongly felt, and sovereignty is jealously guarded, the Member States have always been reluctant to move towards structured forms of defence cooperation, let alone integration. This was true back in 1954, when the French aborted their own plan—the Pleven Plan—to establish a defence community, and has remained so since that day.

Those reservations are still there, but two key variables have changed. Survey upon survey in recent years points to two interesting facts. First, as noted above, Europeans feel increasingly insecure, notwithstanding the different sources of such insecurity. Second, and even more important, they see in a collective effort—the EU—an indispensable component of their security. Majorities in all the Member States would like to see "more Europe" in security and defence (Pew Research Center 2016). At times in which Euroscepticism runs high, broad support for more European foreign and security policy across all the Member States—interestingly including the UK which decided to leave the Union—is notable indeed. And rational it is too: In a space in which goods, services, money and people move freely, security cannot be guaranteed by the Member States acting disjointly.

The Brexit: Fact and Fiction

Third is Brexit. Whereas the UK had been at the forefront of the push towards what eventually became the CSDP in the years following the Franco-British 1998 St Malò Declaration, since the Conservative Party's return to power in 2010, London has become lukewarm if not outright sceptical of the idea of deeper European defence cooperation, let alone integration. The concern, which had always been present in the British body politic, but visibly rose as Euroscepticism escalated under Tory rule, was that stepping up European security and defence work would be to the detriment of the Atlantic Alliance. London believes firmly that NATO is the dominant framework for European defence. The EU could and should play a useful but subsidiary—or in bureaucratic speak "complementary"—role to NATO: NATO should continue to do hard defence, while the EU is welcome to step up its efforts particularly on soft security.

Those who believed instead that the Union should enhance its integration efforts, including in defence, saw in the outcome of the 23 June referendum in the UK a silver lining. Now that the British foot was off the brake of an EU security and defence union, the rest could get on with the business. Personally, I have never been of the view that Europeans could make a meaningful effort on security and defence completely detached from the UK, which alongside France, represents the most credible defence actor in Europe, both in terms of military capabilities and the willingness to use them. Nor have I ever believed that the UK was the only, and on many issues even the strongest, brake on deeper European defence cooperation. There are some specific issues on which the UK has voiced its concerns louder than others. The establishment of a permanent EU operational headquarter for the command and control of EU military operations is a case in point. The idea of an operational headquarter signals to a NATO-first Member State like the UK the risk of duplicating or draining resources from NATO's Supreme Headquarters Allied Powers Europe (SHAPE). But in reality, on those issues on which the UK raised the red flag, it rarely did so alone. It was often joined by others, who either echoed London in speaking out against, or conveniently hid behind the unveiled British threat to veto.

Time will tell if and to what extent the UK was the principal obstacle to European defence integration, whose failure predates the establishment of the European Communities in 1957 and the UK's entry in them in 1973. But politics often acquires a dynamic of its own, at times detached from historical realities and hard facts, particularly in our post-truth political age. In other words, regardless of whether the UK had been the true brake or merely the big alibi for the EU's failures on security and defence, the British people's decision to leave the EU propelled the European security and defence debate to a new level. Realities aside, Brexit had an impact on the European defence debate by feeding the narrative of "now that the British roadblock towards European defence is removed, let the rest get on with it".

The Brexit effect played out at a different level too. The UK referendum sent shock waves across the EU. Since its birth, the EU had only known expansion. In successive waves of enlargement in 1973, in the early 1980s, in 1995, in 2004, 2007 and 2013, the Union progressively grew from six to twenty-eight Member States, at times biting off more than it could chew. The Union was used to the countries knocking at the door, not to the Member States running for the exit. While the possibility had been contemplated with the insertion of Article 50 in the Treaty of Lisbon, the mechanics and modalities of an exit had not been thoroughly thought through, not least because in 2008 no one had foreseen this as a concrete possibility. Now that the UK had chosen to leave, and Eurosceptic populism was on the rise across many Member States, European leaders felt compelled to signal their commitment to European integration. At the informal Bratislava summit of the 27 remaining Heads of State and Government in September 2016, the political imperative was that of sending a strong signal of unity. The 27 regretted the British decision to leave, but they would stand united in moving forward together.

A Political Commission

To this list of reasons concerning why the spotlight turned on security and defence, a final one must be added: the role of the European Commission. The European Commission had been traditionally unwilling to touch defence issues. The "D" word was somewhat of a dirty word in the *Berlaymont*. The limits set by the EU Treaties to fund defence from the EU budget made the Commission, as guardian of the Treaties, doubly sceptical of defence. With the work carried out on the Global Strategy and the full use of the double role of the High Representative as also Vice-President of the European Commission, the European Commission is now fully committed to becoming a player on security and defence. The Commission can provide facilitation and incentives for Europeans to do more and do more together in this field. In November 2016, the European Commission presented a European Defence Action Plan, outlining a set of financial measures to induce the Member States to move towards greater defence cooperation. The most concrete element in this Plan is the launch of a defence research programme, in which the Commission will start funding collaborative defence research projects like it already does in non-defence-related matters under the Horizon 2020 programme. In so far as defence research is among the areas on which Europeans spend the least within their defence budgets and certainly do not spend together, the Commission's Defence Action Plan is a welcome step in the European defence panorama. Another key provision is the idea that Member States' spending on the joint development of defence capabilities would be exempt from the Stability and Growth Pact's rules, of interest particularly to ambitious Eurozone Member States whose hands are tied by the Eurozone's fiscal rules. In short, if realised, the Commission's commitment to put concrete chips on the defence table has represented an important initiative, potentially even a game-changer towards a European defence union.

So, a constellation of demand and supply driven factors meant that the EU's security and defence moment has come, if the Member States manage to seize it. It is a window of political opportunity that may not last long, given the volatile political climate in many Member States. In the light of this, HRVP Mogherini wanted to do her part in seizing the moment. She therefore pressed the accelerator and opted to proceed as rapidly and practically as possible.

During the drafting of the EUGS, many believed that a key component of its follow-up would be an EU "defence white book" (Biscop 2015). By the end of the summer of 2016, the HRVP opted against this approach. A defence white book means different things in different countries. But in most cases, white books are long and detailed, they begin with a threat assessment and then quantify and qualify the defence capabilities needed to address such threats. In nation-states, drawing up a white book generally takes about one year. In the case of the EU, I dare not imagine how long it would have taken. The HRVP was convinced that the Union did not have such time at its disposal. The window of opportunity on European defence would probably not have lasted that long. The approach rapidly turned to the down to earth, practical and pragmatic. The HRVP chose to produce an "Implementation Plan on Security and Defence", a non-descript title which captures the frame of mind she was in. Yes, the EU would need to agree on a new level of ambition on security and defence. The Implementation Plan would therefore need to flesh out the three security and defence tasks highlighted in the EUGS—external crisis response, the building of security and defence capacities of the EU's partners, and the protection of the Union and its citizens. But above all, the EU had to agree on a set of concrete measures to achieve its level of ambition, including through capability development, defence cooperation, a review of the rapid response toolbox, including the yet to be used Battlegroups, an increase of financing, a revision of the EEAS's crisis management structures so as to allow for a more effective planning and conduct of CSDP missions and operations, and, *dulcis in fundo*, the possible activation of a permanent structured cooperation (PESCO) between a core group of the Member States determined to make a step change on EU security and defence. PESCO is a possibility provided for in the Lisbon Treaty, which has not been used to date.

By mid-November, the Implementation Plan was out, welcomed by the Foreign Affairs Council meeting in joint format with Defence Ministers (EU HRVP 2016). The Conclusions of that Council took up the concrete actions in the Implementation Plan, providing an agreed roadmap of the steps ahead (Council of the EU 2016b). Some Member States felt the process had been somewhat rushed. But all recognised that the time to demonstrate unity and ambition on this dossier was then.

The coming months and years will tell whether this was, yet again, a false dawn for a European security and defence union. The EU's history is littered by patiently negotiated common decisions which are then left hanging in mid-air. What was clear though was that in November 2016, the Council took the most ambitious decisions since the birth of the CSDP, and it did so as, and perhaps in some respect because, the entire European edifice was at stake.

Final Thoughts: Lessons Learned from the EU Global Strategy

The European Union is living through its deepest and darkest existential crisis. The Union that my generation grew up with and started taking for granted may not survive. The peace, prosperity and security that my and my parents' generation enjoyed are crumbling before our eyes, risking to become beyond the reach of our children.

Small as a step it may be, the EU Global Strategy and the efforts made on its implementation have sought to galvanise Europeans, through a shared vision, towards common external action. Time will tell whether such efforts will succeed or whether they will be washed away by the wave of nationalism, populism, racism and protectionism gripping Europe, the so-called West, and the wider international system. As Gramsci put it, alluding to the rise of fascism and national socialism in the interwar years: "The old world is dying, and the new world struggles to be born; now is the time of monsters".[2] These indeed are times of monsters.

The internal odds are stacked against success. The Union is in crisis. Multiple and overlapping divisions over the economy and migration have prevented the EU from doing anything but the bare minimum to avoid catastrophe and collapse. Solidarity, trust and empathy between Member States are rock bottom, EU institutions are viewed as ever more detached from the concerns of ordinary citizens, and Brexit has awakened the spectre of disintegration. Europe's woes are, as always, part of a broader global phenomenon. The backlash against globalisation, interdependence and structured partnerships is not limited to Europe, as the United States now knows. But unlike the nation-state, which may survive while arguably not thrive under a wave of closure and nationalism, the EU's very existence is premised on the polar opposite principles being the accepted norm. The EU is based upon openness and cosmopolitanism, and cannot survive without them.

Divisions between Member States have at times polluted foreign policy too. On occasions, some Member States stand out against a specific common foreign policy line. At times, they do so not because they actually take issue with that foreign policy point in and of itself, but rather to make a point on another policy dossier, be it the economy, asylum policy or migration. The point is simply to make the point. Sadly, nowadays there is hardly any political cost – in fact quite the opposite – in being a spoiler within the EU. Euroscepticism is the norm, and Member States – even the theoretically Europhile ones – pride themselves when publically bashing the Union. The broader risk of a negative spill-over from other policy areas onto foreign policy therefore exists. This could happen particularly if the Brexit negotiations were to get nasty and contaminate the foreign policy domain as well, harming the interests of both the EU and the UK. The risk is there, and on occasion it materializes. But it has not become systemic or widespread yet. *The elections in late 2016 and in 2017 in Austria, the Netherlands, France and Germany suggest that the pro-European side holds, though it is being challenged.*

Alongside divisions between the Member States are the pathologies of EU institutions. In principle, the institutions claim they understand the need to get closer to the citizen. Successions of Eurobarometer polls and EU-related referendums are simply too much to ignore. Several of the steps taken by the Juncker Commission seek to tackle head-on the welfare of EU citizens. Yet the awareness, while there in theory, at times struggles to sink in practice. I recall a conversation with a senior Commission official in the spring of 2015, in which he criticised the gloomy picture of the EU presented in the strategic assessment (Annex A). He argued that while populism and Euroscepticism were on the rise, they ultimately represented fringe movements. Appalled at what I was hearing, I suggested to my interlocutor that he might want to take a walk outside *Rondpoint Schuman* to get a glimpse of where Europe is heading. A superficial awareness of the depth of the crisis within the institutions comes alongside a "business as usual" approach to policy practice. And the policy practice of the institutions is made of long and rigid procedures, cumbersome negotiations and, in the best of circumstances, small steps which are hardly visible to the woman in the street. As one colleague put it to me at a conference in the summer of 2016, the mental state of EU institutions harks back to when the Politburo met to discuss agrarian reform as the Soviet Union was collapsing in 1991. The EU in 2016 is not the Soviet Union of 1991. Notwithstanding the frequent institutional turf wars, the difficulty in making bold steps, the religious fixation with procedures and the constant mixing up of process with action, not all is lost. Paradoxically, the dire predicament that Europeans find themselves in could galvanise the necessary political will towards common action. It is precisely the gravity of the external threats and challenges the Union faces and the painful awareness that no one – read the United States – will save us from them that may make foreign policy the one area in which well-known divisions are abated. As argued throughout this book and evidenced by the process leading to the EU Global Strategy, Member States have different concerns and worries. But they are all equally very concerned and very worried, and are all becoming aware that their external woes cannot be addressed by bowling alone. When it comes to foreign policy, including but not limited to security and defence, the EU is a necessity. You may love it or hate it. But regardless of whether you're in Tallinn, Athens, Paris, Berlin, Budapest, Helsinki or Rome, you need it.

This is not to say that the European project will be saved by foreign policy. Unless European leaders manage to agree and implement effective policies to address key challenges in the areas of economy and migration, the Union is unlikely to survive the wave of populist Euroscepticism spreading like wildfire across the continent. EU foreign policy, and the EUGS as a key case of it, can at best represent a small contribution to keeping the Union alive in the meantime. But the EUGS should not be viewed as the European equivalent of the Soviet Union's agrarian reform in 1991. The Global Strategy is not the swansong of the Union. The strategic reflection, the EUGS and its follow-up, demonstrates that Europeans can still be united and do appreciate, now more than ever, the need to be so in foreign policy. If, as, and when Europeans act together in the world because there simply is no alternative in the twenty-first century, time will hopefully come in which that same sense of unity will be rediscovered and be put to the service of a re-founded Union as a whole.

NOTES

1. Conversation with one of the pen holders of the ESS, May 2015.
2. Original: "*il Vecchio mondo sta morendo. Quello nuovo tarda a comparire. E in questo chiaroscuro, nascono i mostri*".

REFERENCES

Bendiek, Annegret. 2016. *The Global Strategy for the EU's Foreign and Security Policy*. SWP Comments No. 38. Berlin: SWP.https://www.swp-berlin.org/fileadmin/contents/products/comments/2016C38_bdk.pdf.

Biscop, Sven. 2015. Out of the Blue: A White Book. *European Geostrategy* 7 (71). https://www.europeangeostrategy.org/2015/11/out-of-the-blue-a-white-book.

Biscop, Sven. 2016. *The EU Global Strategy: Realpolitik with European Characteristics*. Security Policy Brief No. 75. Brussels: Egmont, July.https://www.egmontinstitute.be/wp-content/uploads/2016/06/SPB75.pdf.

Colemont, Jo. 2016. The EUGS: Realistic, but Not Too Modest Please. *The International Spectator* 51 (3): 9–11. doi:10.1080/03932729.2016.1217608.

Council of the EU. 2016a. *Council Conclusions on the Global Strategy on the European Union's Foreign and Security Policy Adopted by the Council at its 3492nd Meeting Held on 17 October 2016*.https://www.data.consilium.europa.eu/doc/document/ST-13202-2016-INIT/en/pdf.

Council of the EU. 2016b. *Council Conclusions on Implementing the EU Global Strategy in the Area of Security and Defence, Adopted by the Council at its 3498th Meeting Held on 14 November 2016*. https://data.consilium.europa.eu/doc/document/ST-14149-2016-INIT/en/pdf.

Dijkstra, Hylke, ed. 2016. Forum: The EU Global Strategy. *Contemporary Security Policy*, 37 (3): 369–472.

European Council. 2003. *Presidency Conclusions*. Brussels, 12–13 December.https://www.consilium.europa.eu/uedocs/cms_data/docs/pressdata/en/ec/78364.pdf.

EU High Representative. 2003. *A Secure Europe in a Better World. European Security Strategy*. December. https://www.consilium.europa.eu/uedocs/cmsUpload/78367.pdf.

EU HRVP. 2016. *Implementation Plan on Security and Defence*. 14 November.https://eeas.europa.eu/sites/eeas/files/eugs_implementation_plan_st14392.en16_0.pdf.

Juncos, Ana E. 2016. Resilience as the New EU Foreign Policy Paradigm: A Pragmatist Turn? *European Security* 26 (1): 1–18. doi:10.1080/09662839.2016.1247809.

Mações, Bruno. 2016. Facing the World, Together and Apart. Europe's World 33 (Autumn).https://europesworld.org/?p=11358.

Maull, Hans W. 2016. Sadly, the EUGS Reads More like a Symptom of the Problem than Part of a Solution for Europe's Deep Crisis. *The International Spectator* 51 (3): 34–36. doi:10.1080/03932729.2016.1217071.

Pew Research Center. 2016. *Europeans Face the World Divided*. Pew Survey, June.https://pewrsr.ch/1WIdvUf.

Smith, Michael E. 2016. Implementing the Global Strategy Where It Matters Most: The EU's Credibility Deficit and the European Neighbourhood.

Contemporary Security Policy 37 (3): 446–460. doi:10.1080/13523260.201
6.1240467.

Techau, Jan. 2016. The EU's New Global Strategy: Useful or Pointless? *Strategic
Europe*, 1 July. https://carnegieeurope.eu/strategiceurope/?fa=63994.

Ülgen, Sinan. 2016. Resilience as the Guiding Principle of EU External Action.
Strategic Europe, 5 July. https://carnegieeurope.eu/strategiceurope/
?fa=64007.

Wagner, Wolfgang, and Rosanne Anholt. 2016. Resilience as the EU
Global Strategy's New Leitmotif: Pragmatic, Problematic or Promising?
Contemporary Security Policy 37 (3): 414–430. doi:10.1080/13523260.201
6.1228034.

Annex A:
The European Union in a Changing Global Environment:
A More Connected, Contested and Complex World

We used to think that Europe had *"never been so prosperous,* so *secure* nor so free"* With much of the previous century having been marred by turmoil on the continent and in the wider world, the turn of the millennium was indeed a high-water mark. Much has been achieved since 2003: the EU has integrated 13 new members, fostered stability in the Western Balkans and contributed to peacebuilding in Africa and elsewhere. Yet the overriding perception now is that Europe's prosperity has been hit by economic crises, and that its security and freedoms are openly under threat.

Today, the EU is surrounded by an arc of instability. To the east, basic tenets of international law, such as the inviolability of borders, are no longer respected. In the Middle East, the unravelling of a century-old regional order has unleashed war and human suffering. As states collapse and regional powers collide, terrorists spread fear and destruction throughout the region, connecting to networks in Africa and on European soil. Further afield, we see global and regional players jostling for influence in Asia, while climate change and an increased competition for scarce natural resources risk generating further conflict in many parts of the world.

At the same time, global growth, interdependence, connectivity and technological progress are enabling ever more people to escape poverty and live longer, healthier and freer lives. Growing numbers of citizens around the world aspire to a way of life based on democratic institutions, human rights and the rule of law. Indeed, while there has been

© The Editor(s) (if applicable) and The Author(s) 2017

N. Tocci, *Framing the EU Global Strategy*, Palgrave Studies in European Union Politics, DOI 10.1007/978-3-319-55586-7 a remarkable diffusion of international human rights norms and mechanisms in recent decades, the protection of human rights has not been implemented across the board. A more connected world brings such paradoxes to the fore.

When faced with this world of disorder and of opportunity, two things are clear. First, global trends are neither linear nor preordained, but often the product of shocks and human choices. This highlights the uncertainty that lies ahead, but also the role of agency—including that of the EU—in moving forward. We may not fully know our future, but we can shape it. Second, the EU does not have the luxury of turning inwards. We have a responsibility to protect our citizens, while promoting our interests and universal values. It is a responsibility dictated by history and an interest dictated by geography. The very nature of the EU as a construct of intertwined polities gives us a unique advantage to help steer the way in a more complex, more connected but also more contested world.

A Changing Global Environment

A More Connected World

Globalisation has been the dominant force shaping our world for the best part of the last century. Today, it is giving rise to an unprecedented degree of connectivity. Global connectivity is changing the meaning of borders. A surge in human mobility—from tourists to terrorists, from students to refugees—compels us to change how we think about migration, citizenship, health and development. Global tourism is expected to approach 2 billion by 2030. Migration along south–south—and to a lesser extent south–north—routes is accelerating as a result of conflict, repression, economic disparity, demographic imbalances and climate change. Extremists, too, exploit the opportunities arising from porous borders: the numbers of "foreign terrorist fighters" estimated to have travelled to Syria and Iraq far exceed those that had waged *jihad* in Afghanistan, Iraq or Somalia in the past. With greater mobility also comes the risk of greater spread of pandemics. The Ebola outbreak is the latest, but surely not the last, manifestation (Fig. A.1).

A more connected world also comes as a result of the exponential surge and spread of webs. By 2030, Internet users are expected to near 5

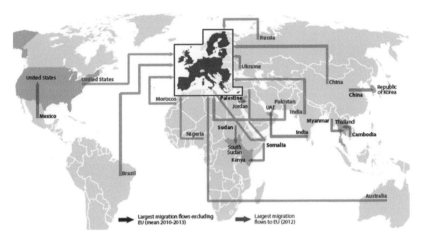

Fig. A.1 Global migration flows. *Source* EUISS (from Eurostat data; IOM World Migration Report 2013)

billion. By then, 80% of the world's population will have mobile connectivity and 60% will enjoy broadband access. Big data, data mining, cloud computing and the Internet of Things will shape the pace and contours of how we live, work and consume. The digital age offers tremendous benefits to billions of people in terms of wealth, knowledge and freedom. As such, the security and stability of the net, as well as the integrity of data flows, is of growing importance to our economies and our societies. Communication technologies have already had profound political impact, mobilising millions in Tahrir and Maidan. The fight to protect the freedom of and on the net is thus becoming increasingly critical for the protection and promotion of human rights throughout the world. However, technology also creates new vulnerabilities, including opportunities for *jihadists* and traffickers of arms, drugs and human beings, as well as for public and private actors to engage in counterfeiting and financial and economic crime. Globalisation empowers individuals—for good or ill (Fig. A.2).

Markets too are increasingly connected. Geo-economics—the global competition for access to markets and resources—has become a key driver of international relations. Examples include China's efforts to develop infrastructural ties with Central and Southeast Asia as well as Europe, the growth of regional and sub-regional groupings in East Asia

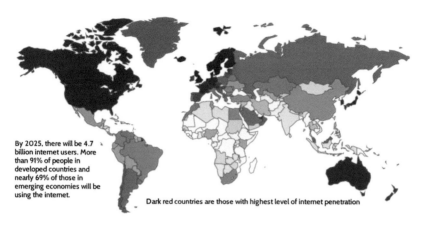

By 2025, there will be 4.7 billion internet users. More than 91% of people in developed countries and nearly 69% of those in emerging economies will be using the internet.

Dark red countries are those with highest level of internet penetration

Fig. A.2 Percentage of individuals using the Internet. *Source* International Telecommunication Union data, 2013

and sub-Saharan Africa, or the Trans-Pacific Partnership negotiations. A rising Asia is now the most dynamic element of the global economy. At the same time, we face an "Asian paradox": while the region's economy is buoyed by integration and sense of optimism, strategic competition among regional powers is feeding concern about a fragmented security environment. Similar paradoxes also exist in other parts of the world.

If the world is more connected than at any point in the past, the same is true for the European Union. The EU has expanded from 15 to 28 Member States, and the Lisbon Treaty has generated opportunities to better integrate EU security and defence policies with external relation policies. The Eurozone crisis has highlighted the interconnections and asymmetries within the Union and demonstrated that the crisis could only be addressed through greater integration. The last 5 years have seen steps forward in economic governance which were previously unthinkable. At the same time, the EU is moving towards building an Energy Union to tackle fragmented energy markets through more effective coordination of energy policies and new investments in critical infrastructure. Likewise, the EU is making progress in creating a digital single market and deepening integration and investment in R&D.

These developments have profound implications for the Union's foreign policy. The Eurozone crisis temporarily tarnished the EU's international reputation and took a toll on its self-confidence and openness to the outside world. Europeans have since been concerned with jobs and growth, while developing less of an appetite for expensive endeavours abroad. At the same time, steps forward in economic governance are putting the crisis behind us, and the European way of life continues to attract tourists, businesses, students and migrants. Efforts to build an Energy Union will help rebalance relations with Russia, the Caucasus and the Middle East. The political economy of defence, coupled with security crises beyond the EU's borders, could lead to deeper cooperation between the Member States, and thereby boost the Common Security and Defence Policy (CSDP). This, in turn, would help bolster partnerships with the UN, NATO and regional organisations.

A More Contested World

We used to think that greater interdependence would automatically bring about peace and prevent war. Now we know that while a more connected world is full of opportunities, it is also putting the nation state under unprecedented strain. By generating vulnerabilities and fragmented identities, this is giving rise to tensions and, at times, leading to more conflict. It is becoming a more dangerous world.

Fragile states and ungoverned spaces are becoming more widespread. Nowhere is this clearer than closest to home. To the east, our neighbours suffer from economic, political and energy-related vulnerabilities. Russia has actively destabilised some of them by undermining their freedom, sovereignty and security. Beyond the imperative of fostering democracy, human rights (including the rights of minorities) and good governance, the conflict over Ukraine underlines the need to bolster the statehood prerogatives of our neighbours. These include recognised and protected borders, a sustainable fiscal capacity, as well as functioning customs services and police and military forces. What is at stake is peace on our continent.

Across the Mediterranean, the spread of ungoverned spaces from Libya to Syria and Iraq has enabled criminals, extremists and terrorists to thrive. Yet a repressive state is no recipe for long-term stability. The value of the few fragile democracies in the region, with Tunisia in the lead, should not be underestimated. It is crucial to recall that political change does not happen overnight and that progress is often accompanied by setbacks. Further south—from the Sahel to the Horn, from the Great Lakes to the Gulf of Guinea—instability and violence are the products of poverty, corruption, human rights abuses and conflict-ridden electoral politics. Although casualties on the battlefield have decreased significantly over time, we have seen a dramatic rise in civilian victims and refugees: more than 50 million people are displaced worldwide. The consequences of this human tragedy will reverberate across regions and generations—including within the EU.

Identity and ideology fuel tensions on different continents. Both in Europe and in the wider world, the model of an open society is being questioned and other concepts put forward. In the Middle East, identity politics makes for an explosive mix—from the deeply entrenched Israeli–Palestinian conflict to the rivalry between Saudi Arabia and Iran, which is aggravating sectarianism across the region. Moreover, a crisis of unprecedented magnitude has broken out inside the Sunni world, revolving around different interpretations of political Islam. And violent extremism—in various incarnations and franchises—feeds on grievances, repression and despair across the Middle East, North Africa and large swathes of sub-Saharan Africa and Asia. There is also a growing danger of proliferation of weapons of mass destruction (WMD) and advanced conventional weapons across the Middle East and Asia.

Demographic trends threaten to increase the risk of conflict in years to come. The global population, standing at 7.2 billion today, is expected to grow to 9.6 billion by 2050. More than half of the world's demographic growth will come from Africa. At the same time, Africa's GDP is expected to remain five times lower than China's and half that of India, which will exacerbate poverty and could raise the risk of mass displacement and radicalisation. While Africa's natural resources and growing workforce create ample opportunities, the continent's potential will only be realised if efforts related to job creation, good governance, human rights protection and conflict resolution become more effective.

By 2030, the global middle class is expected to rise to 5 billion. But inequalities are set to rise too, in both the developed and the developing worlds, potentially triggering social discontent. The new global middle class is likely to be less homogenous and more volatile than the Western middle classes of the past. Disparities in wealth, education, digital connectivity and employment opportunities (notably for the young) harbour the potential for greater social mobility, as well as conflict.

Climate change and resource scarcity, coupled with demographic growth, contribute to international conflicts and are expected to do so even more in the future. Climate-induced floods, droughts, desertification and farmland destruction have triggered migration and conflict from Darfur to Mali. Food price hikes in the 2000s triggered riots from Cameroon to Bangladesh and were a factor behind the 2011 Arab uprisings. Meanwhile, water management has become more contentious, with projects such as the Grand Renaissance Dam in Ethiopia and the Rogun Dam in Tajikistan causing regional tensions. By 2025, climate change is expected to slash harvests and water supplies, affecting some 1.4 billion people. Climate change, coupled with demographic growth, will therefore require innovative agricultural solutions: agricultural output will have to increase by 70% in order to feed the planet in 2050. Rising temperatures are also accelerating the melting of glaciers. This could have devastating consequences for coastal regions which are inhabited by 60% of the global population lives. At the same time, the thawing of the glaciers will bring access to new energy, mineral and fishing resources, calling for collective responses to manage access to shipping routes and prevent irreversible environmental damage.

New energy discoveries and technologies can both help address scarcities and bolster efforts to mitigate climate change. Today, we live in times of significant oil over-supply. While the current drop in oil prices is a boon for consumers and energy importers, it threatens the sustainability of many energy-producing countries. By 2035, however, energy consumption is expected to rise by over 40% compared to 2012, with 95% coming from emerging economies. Energy security and climate change will thus remain a global challenge for years to come.

Technological progress is also changing the nature of conflict. Big data and cloud technology are revolutionising the defence industry and may open new avenues for crisis management. Dual-use technology has been critical in advancing scientific research and industrial development. But it could also favour the proliferation of WMDs and the development of sophisticated conventional arms such as lethal autonomous weapon systems. The surge in Internet users has made cybercrime and terrorist use of the Internet a new frontier of twenty-first-century warfare. Terrorists use information and communication technologies to recruit, finance, intimidate and disseminate their message. The conflict over Ukraine has exposed the hybrid nature of destabilisation, which combines twentieth-century conventional warfare with twenty-first-century tactics. These include the jamming of command, control and strategic communications systems, cyber espionage and disinformation campaigns, covert operations, foreign asset acquisitions, the disruption of critical infrastructure, encouraging corruption and trade- and energy-related coercion. We are certainly more connected, but not always and not necessarily more secure.

The European Union, too, is more contested. The financial and economic crisis has posed a serious challenge to European unity. Many Europeans have been hit by the crisis and have come to view themselves as losers of globalisation. This is feeding certain constituencies within the Member States which express criticism of, if not outright opposition to, the European project. This trend, which often blends legitimate grievances with a dangerous mix of nationalism, populism, protectionism and even racism, is exposing a new rift within the EU and bringing new anti-establishment forces to the fore. It is a divide between elites and citizens manifested in voter disaffection, and a lack of trust in public institutions and policies. It is a divide among citizens driven by unemployment, strained welfare systems, unsuccessful migration and integration policies, as well as by terrorism and radicalisation. And it is a generational divide driven by youth unemployment and exclusion. All this is adding to the pressure for greater differentiation within the EU. While differentiation has long been a fact of EU life, it has become a more prominent and possibly more permanent feature of the Union.

A more contested EU is bringing about broader external challenges. The rise of nationalism, protectionism and illiberalism could expose European nations to the lure of anti-democratic models promoted from outside. Populism and racism could feed fortress Europe mentalities, undermining credible enlargement and neighbourhood policies, forthcoming migration and mobility policies and even trade liberalisation. Radicalisation requires the EU to put a premium not only on enhanced border management, data protection, Internet governance and intelligence cooperation, but also on efforts to improve education and community dialogue.

And yet, a more contested EU also represents an opportunity for change. The Union is committed to regaining lost confidence, supporting those that have suffered most during the crisis and rekindling trust in disenfranchised Europeans. Plans aimed at promoting investment, economic growth and job creation are part of this determined effort. If well managed, internal differentiation could help accommodate differences within the EU and revamp enlargement and neighbourhood policies. It could help transform the divisive "all-or-nothing" membership question into a more constructive "integration" question—based on successive functional building blocks—to the benefit of all. A self-questioning EU can also spur decision makers to connect foreign policy with citizens' expectations. And it can inject new energy in the European debate through a generational change in politics. The onus is upon us to forge a new social contract with European citizens also through foreign policy.

A More Complex World

We live in an age of power shifts at a global level and power diffusion at all levels—away from governments and towards markets, media, civil (and less civil) societies and individuals.

A dose of nuanced realism is required. Despite much talk of America's decline, in 2030 the USA will probably still enjoy its global economic, military, technological and financial reach. With a global currency and an unrivalled set of alliances, this places the USA in a pivotal position to shape world affairs into the twenty-first century. Likewise, while no single EU country is likely to have an economy justifying G7 membership by 2050, the Union is set to retain one of the highest per capita incomes in the world. The EU has all the means to be an influential global player in future—if it acts together.

Still, the age of dominance by any single country or group of countries, experienced first by European colonial powers and then the USA, is over. The combined effect of rising literacy, jobs and disposable incomes, along with the accelerating rate of technological progress, is expanding the number of stakeholders in world affairs.

Prime among the "new" powers is China, whose rise is reversing a two-century-long historical anomaly. With an average growth of 10% over the last two decades (now settling at more moderate levels), China has already lifted 600 million people out of poverty. By 2030, China's GDP is expected to represent 20% of the world's total, overtaking that of both the EU and the USA. China's military spending is growing fast and its economic, security and social reach is rising, notably in Asia and Africa. However, even if it continued on current trends and surpassed the USA in absolute terms within a couple of decades, China would struggle to reach US-level military capabilities. Next comes India, set to account for 16% of the world's GDP by 2030. By 2045, India will probably spend as much on defence as all EU Member States combined, and by 2050, China and India's combined GDP may overtake that of the entire OECD. Among the "BRICS", Russia belongs in a different category, mostly due to a bleaker economic and demographic future. Nevertheless, its defence spending has increased by 30% since 2008. Other powers like Brazil, Mexico, Indonesia, South Korea, Nigeria, South Africa and Turkey are all likely to rise in global power rankings (Figs. A.3 and A.4).

The rise of other powers is undeniable. Less certain is whether they will form a single cohesive alternative bloc. The creation of the BRICS Development Bank and China's Asian Infrastructure and Investment Bank, the current Sino-Russian rapprochement, and the sensitivities of some large democracies at the UN regarding atrocity prevention and the international promotion of human rights seem to corroborate this prospect. But the reality is messier. Rising powers argue that the post-World War II order needs to be reformed, but they are divided or uncertain about the precise changes they would like to see. They share a pragmatic approach to foreign policy, but each rising power is following its own path to modernity. Profound divergences between their political systems remain, and in many respects, they are strategic competitors. In short, emerging powers lack a key ingredient of lasting cooperation: a common system of values or interests to bind them into a cohesive force.

Moreover, different regions display different configurations of powers that do not add up to a single coherent whole. In the Middle East, Russia and China are increasingly active, but the real game-changer is

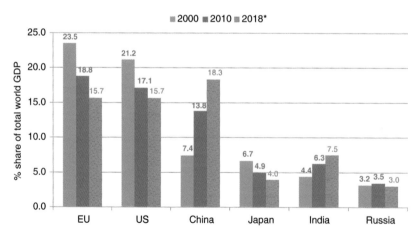

Fig. A.3 GDP share of world total (%). *Source* IMF, WEO (Oct. 2014) | *Note* GDP is adjusted for Purchasing Power Parity (PPP) | *IMF forecast based on current trends

Fig. A.4 Shifting centre of gravity of the world economy. *Source* McKinsey Global Institute

the central role played by the Gulf States, Iran and Turkey. The competition between regional actors stretches into the Horn of Africa in what has become an interdependent Red Sea sub-region. In Asia, a China-only focus does not fully capture regional dynamics: the strategic landscape is more complicated. In Africa, growth has reduced the continent's willingness to import rules, norms and practices passively from outside. While global powers—notably the USA, the EU and China—play prominent roles, Africans increasingly steer the continent's affairs. In Latin America, Brazil and Mexico are the major economic players, but Argentina, Colombia and others could form a "middle class" of powers, albeit not united in purpose yet. Across regional theatres, there is no single set of powers with roughly equal influence everywhere—nor are regional hegemons determining dynamics on their own. Power configurations change across time and place, making regions themselves dynamic concepts. The world system is no longer bipolar, unipolar or even multipolar: the very notion of "polarity" is in question.

Adding to such complexity is the shift from a world of nation states to a networked globe of state, non-state, inter-state and transnational actors—from civil society, media and business to regional, sub-regional and mini-lateral groupings. While nation states will remain the basic building blocks of the international system, their national sovereignty is increasingly contested and constrained by the connectivity and complexity within and across different world regions. We live in a world of multiple players and layers bound by complex interdependence. We live in a world of overlapping webs, in which power no longer resides within actors but circulates among them.

We know that variable geometries of state and non-state actors will shape the world in new ways. What we do not know are the rules of global interaction and who will set them. The global power shift and power diffusion are challenging traditional multilateralism. While the UN remains the principal guarantor of the sovereign equality among states, the composition of its Security Council and the distribution of voting rights in the International Financial Institutions no longer reflect current realities. The World Trade Organisation has grown in membership (and thus legitimacy), but not in ability to achieve consensus or advance multilateral trade liberalisation.

The G20 has emerged as a major informal forum, reflecting global power realignments. But while it played a key role in short-term crisis management during the 2008 financial crisis, it has failed so far to tackle structural global challenges in economic growth, financial markets and development. No effective global institutions are in place to confront other pressing challenges such as migration, cyber security, arms control or natural resource management. Opposing existing global governance mechanisms has been easier than creating new ones.

Historically, major power transitions have been accompanied by military conflict. The current challenge is to facilitate a peaceful transition towards a new global order which reflects universal values and in which the interests of all stakeholders are respected within the confines of agreed rules. This new system needs to take into account the global power shift and power diffusion. It will need to tackle a world which is at once more integrated and connected, but also more fragmented and contested. While remaining anchored in the UN, the new system is likely to be more flexible and multifaceted than envisaged by the aspirations which underpinned the post-World War II architecture. In a world of incalculable risk and opportunity, crafting effective responses will hinge on the ability to adjust, react and innovate in partnership with others.

CHALLENGES AND OPPORTUNITIES FOR THE EU

A more connected, contested and complex global environment has different regional manifestations. In the emerging global environment, the EU is faced with five broad sets of challenges and opportunities.

Redoubling Commitment to Our European Neighbours

In eastern and south-eastern Europe, the EU retains substantial influence and is able to generate positive change. Enlargement produced remarkable transformations in acceding Member States. The EU has been instrumental in bringing about the stabilisation and demilitarisation of the Western Balkans and the Serbia-Kosovo dialogue. It was also critical in fostering reforms in Turkey. Beyond enlargement, the EU's power of attraction persists in parts of the eastern neighbourhood.

But the EU's "soft power" is waning as the memory of the "big bang" enlargement recedes and other actors strive for influence in its neighbourhood. Today's challenge is to revive the reform momentum through credible policies of integration and association. In the Western Balkans, promoting economic integration and development are essential to counter de-industrialisation, unemployment and low investment. In Turkey, the task is to rekindle a positive political reform dynamic and move forward on structural economic reforms. In those eastern neighbours seeking closer ties with the EU, the Union has a unique role to play to support political, economic, governance and broader societal reform.

At the same time, the conflict over Ukraine, Russia's hybrid destabilisation tactics, Europe's energy security challenges and Turkey's rise as a regional power all highlight—in different ways and to different degrees—the imperative of forging a genuine common foreign policy that includes but is not limited to an accession or association policy.

The EU must indeed "develop a special relationship with neighbouring countries". But this does not necessarily mean that enlargement and the European Neighbourhood Policy are the only ways of doing so. Our approach to Turkey cannot neglect issues of common interest, including trade, migration, energy and security in the region. Our approach towards our eastern partners needs to include robust policies to prevent and resolve conflict, bolster statehood along with economic development, and foster energy and transport connectivity. And our policy towards Russia needs to prevent new dividing lines by combining a firm response to destabilising actions at and within our borders with engagement to rebuild a sustainable European security order with which all are at ease, while seeking common approaches to global issues.

Rethinking the EU's Approach Towards North Africa and the Middle East (MENA)

The positive human energy unleashed by the 2011 Arab uprisings has given way to a wave of upheavals in the region, featuring collapsing states, thriving terrorist networks, burgeoning transnational crime, millions of refugees and intolerable violence. All this, too, is happening at our doorstep, just a few kilometres from our shores.

The most immediate task is that of stemming the tide of terrorists and criminal networks by enhancing the coherence between internal and external security policies. We also have to address the humanitarian crises in war-torn and refugee-hosting countries through humanitarian assistance, asylum policies and development cooperation. In doing so, we must insist on the full application of international humanitarian law, the protection of civilians and the respect of human rights in conflict situations. Our diplomatic, economic, migration, asylum and security policies need to account for the deep connections between Europe's southern neighbours and their neighbours in the Gulf and sub-Saharan Africa in order to help put out the fires ravaging the region, from Libya to Syria, and Iraq to Yemen.

But the biggest challenge is reminding ourselves that stability is no substitute for sustainability and that the root causes of resentment—from repression and deprivation to the "old" Israeli–Palestinian conflict—have deepened across the region. We need to devise policies that, without preaching, support human dignity, social inclusiveness, political responsiveness, educational modernisation and the rule of law across the region. In this respect, devising tailor-made policies in the fields of economic development, social protection and youth inclusion, as well as political accountability, justice and security is key. Equally important is to encourage inclusive and rules-bound reconciliation in old and new conflicts embedded within a new regional security architecture in the wider Middle Eastern space.

Redefining our Relationship with Africa

As in large parts of the MENA region, poverty, food insecurity, ill-governance and conflict continue to plague parts of Africa today. But Africa is also a continent of opportunity and growth, rich in natural resources and agricultural potential. Representative and accountable government is becoming more the norm, and the call for strong institutions, not strong men, is reflected in increasingly credible, albeit in some cases contested, elections. In a world in which key universal values are being questioned, Africa's potential is significant. The secret of success in Africa lies in triggering a virtuous circle in the development–security–migration nexus, bearing in mind the tight interconnections between North and sub-Saharan Africa, as well as between the Horn and the Persian Gulf.

For the EU, Africa has a huge potential for trade, energy and investment, which at the same time is what the continent needs. Likewise, while Europe is facing a daunting demographic predicament, Africa is living through a youth bulge which is expected to persist for most of this century. The resulting equilibrium between demand and supply of migratory forces could either benefit both continents or generate economic strain and political unrest. The EU can help unlock Africa's potential by developing the right mix of migration, mobility and integration policies; by bolstering security cooperation with the UN, the African Union and other African partners; by supporting education and sustainable development; by bridging fair trade and economic integration objectives and by favouring sustainable agriculture and green growth. This can drive Africa's entrepreneurial spirit, and unleash faster, more balanced and sustainable growth while offering more attractive prospects than those provided by other external players. The post-2015 agenda and the 2015 global climate deal could help the EU establish a fairer partnership with Africa, together with a revised post-2020 EU-ACP Partnership.

Reviving Atlantic Partnerships

The global power shift highlights the risk of a structural transatlantic drift. Yet there is an unprecedented presence and demand for more European engagement across world regions, most of all in the Americas. As an overall middle-income region, the successful efforts to overcome entrenched conflicts, the march to democracy, socio-economic progress and the fundamental values we share make the countries of the Americas partners of choice for Europe when tackling global challenges. The complexity and connectivity of our times are enhancing interactions in the wider Atlantic space, and the EU has only to tap this potential.

The transatlantic bond with the USA and Canada is unique and rests on solid political, cultural, economic and security foundations. The opportunity before us is to develop an even stronger and sounder relationship, in which the assets of all are developed and put at the service of common interests. With regard to the USA, security and the economy are two pillars which merit further deepening. In security terms, this means that the EU and its Member States are called to shoulder more responsibility for their neighbourhood, and further develop European defence capabilities. At the same time, as NATO refocuses on territorial defence, CSDP can work with NATO to sharpen its focus on crisis management and hybrid threats. In economic terms, the Transatlantic Trade and Investment Partnership (TTIP) is a potentially win-win project that can create jobs and business opportunities, eliminate red tape and thus stimulate growth. An ambitious and open TTIP would not just be a free-trade and investment agreement. It would be a strategic endeavour that, by establishing the largest free-trade area in the world, may inject momentum into the development of global rules in areas where multilateral negotiations have stalled.

Expanding Atlantic cooperation also means deepening relations with Latin America and the Caribbean through bilateral partnerships, inter-regional relations and in multilateral fora. There is more EU investment in Latin America than in Russia, India and China combined, while cultural ties and migratory flows are strong in both directions. Steps to strengthen ties with individual countries and with organisations such as CELAC, SICA, CARICOM, MERCOSUR and UNASUR reflect these trends.

A Rounded Approach to Asia

The EU has a strategic interest in playing a fully fledged role in and with Asia. The EU has a huge stake in the continued success of Asian economies, including China's reform efforts. But the EU is also vulnerable to the ramifications of underlying political and security tensions. Disputes and conflicts in the region would affect trade routes, financial flows and a regional order in a part of the world which is of paramount importance to the EU.

The challenge ahead is to maximise economic opportunities and access to growth in the region, while positioning the EU as a committed and constructive political and security actor. The EU can tap into the growth of Asia's middle class, while supporting the region in dealing with the environmental and social challenges this brings about. On the back of its own experience, the EU is well placed to offer customised support to regional cooperation efforts in Asia, without preaching a single model. The relationship with ASEAN, as a fellow partner in integration, holds special promise in a region affected by growing geopolitical tensions. The EU can also step up its engagement with regional security structures, fostering a rules-based approach to conflict management. Lastly, the EU should seize the opportunity presented by Asia's multifaceted connectivity drive—from ASEAN's plans to China's "Silk Road Economic Belt and New Maritime Silk Road"—through a multi-pronged approach which brings together various sectoral instruments. It also needs to ensure that these initiatives comply with WTO rules, open public procurement practices and stringent environmental and social standards.

IMPLICATIONS

To be secure, prosperous and free, the EU needs to respond to the challenges and opportunities the global environment presents. Crafting an effective response hinges on the EU's ability to make choices and prioritise areas where it wants to and can make a difference. This also requires that the EU can agree and commit to a set of goals to be pursued through collective action. Lastly, it depends on whether the EU's external action instruments, woven together with the fine thread of diplomacy, are fit for purpose. Taken together, are the EU tools and policies equipped for the task?

An overview of the EU's major external action instruments and policies

- The *Common Foreign and Security Policy* (CFSP) is a tested framework for the EU's collective external action, including support for human rights and democracy, arms control and disarmament, mass atrocity and conflict prevention, mediation, regional strategies and strategic partnerships.
- *Common Security and Defence Policy* (CSDP), with its civilian and military crisis management missions, and its contribution to the development of Member States' capabilities, notably through the European Defence Agency, is a key instrument for external action. It has provided value added to institutional reform and capacity-building initiatives through specialisation in training and mentoring. Several action tracks are programmed to enhance the security–development nexus in capacity building missions, in line with the "comprehensive approach".
- In *counterterrorism* (CT) and *countering violent extremism* (CVE), the EU is crystallising a two-pronged approach: countering radicalisation internally and externally through a narrative based on respect for human rights, diversity and respect for religion; and a criminal justice approach embedded in a security and defence policy framework based on strengthening the judicial, policing and intelligence capacities of partners, in full respect of human rights.
- On *cyber issues* the EU the aims to address threats to the free and open internet, allow EU citizens and businesses to benefit from the digital economy, and put ICT at the service of development, all in respect of the EU's values. Globally, the EU strives for an open and secure cyber realm, in which cyber issues are firmly anchored within the framework of human rights, rule of law and international law.
- In *development cooperation* and *humanitarian assistance*, while traditional goals—the eradication of poverty, the preservation of life and the alleviation of suffering, respectively—remain in place, the approach towards achieving them is evolving. The EU's Agenda for Change emphasised human rights, democracy and good governance along with sustainability and inclusive growth.

It also shifted attention from funding inputs to development outputs. Today, attention is focused on adopting a post-2015 agenda and Sustainable Development Goals (SDGs) in order to eradicate extreme poverty and address all dimensions of sustainable development by using realistic and measurable targets.

- *Trade*, pursued through bilateral and multilateral agreements, has long been recognised as an engine for growth and jobs, as well as helping to promote other goals including human rights, development, energy security and environmental protection.
- In *migration* policy, the EU has a border cooperation agency (FRONTEX), an agency supporting Member States in the field of Asylum (EASO), a new Europol-run intelligence centre aimed at countering migrant smuggling, as well as an Asylum, Migration and Integration Fund. The EU can offer market access, assistance and mobility to neighbouring countries and has been rolling out regional protection programmes to help nearby states absorb refugee flows. The EU is also strengthening cooperation with origin countries through dialogues in the context of the Rabat, Khartoum, Budapest and Prague processes. Collective action is being taken to save lives and cope with mounting pressures through increased solidarity, intelligence sharing and partnerships with transit and origin countries, as well as with the international community.
- In *climate* policy, the EU emission trading scheme has become a cornerstone in the effort to combat climate change and reduce industrial greenhouse gasses, and the EU is committed to achieving a binding agreement at COP21 and bilateral cooperation on resource-efficient and green growth. The Energy Security Strategy and the Energy Union Communication chart the way ahead in *energy* policy. To enhance energy security, much of the answer lies within the EU. But the internal–external nexus in the energy security puzzle is critical, too. Hence, the imperative to diversify energy sources and routes through partnerships with suppliers and transit states.
- A review of the *European Neighbourhood Policy* (ENP) is underway in the light of the developments to the EU's east and south. Two major questions stand out. Geographically, the ENP is confronted with the differences between and within each region,

as well as the tight interlinkages—for good or ill—between the EU's neighbours and the neighbours' own neighbouring countries and regions. Conceptually, the ENP was premised on the notion of "enlargement lite", the relevance and effectiveness of which are now being called into question.

- *Enlargement* has been one of the EU's most successful endeavours. In the early 1990s, the predicament of many eastern neighbours was no different from that of most Central and eastern European Member States: within a generation, the gap between them has widened dramatically. Today, enlargement remains central in EU policy towards the Western Balkans and Turkey.

Challenges in the EU's External Action Instruments

The EU's external action instruments are faced with five major challenges: direction, flexibility, leverage, coordination and capability. Meeting these is essential if the EU is to punch its weight in the wider world.

First is policy *direction*. In recent years, the EU has started updating the direction of its external engagement, and efforts are underway to bring its status within international organisations in line with the Lisbon Treaty. But much more remains to be done.

In CSFP, while in some areas the direction of policy is clear, in others the EU has lost salience and momentum. The "strategic partnerships" require a sharper definition of how to maximise EU influence. In disarmament and arms control, the EU remains anchored to treaty-based commitments and to renewing efforts aimed at revitalising multilateral negotiating bodies. However, the 2005 EU strategy to combat the illicit accumulation and trafficking of small arms and light weapons and their ammunition was conceived in a post-Cold War environment. It is yet to adapt in order to respond to twenty-first-century realities, including the use of conventional weapons by terrorists and criminals, as well as by rebel forces, militias and other non-state actors.

Similarly, in CSDP, although the December 2013 European Council underlined that "defence matters", the current level of ambition and capability targets are not tailored to the changing strategic environment, featuring hybrid threats, intertwined internal and external security challenges and the growing need for Europeans to take responsibility for their own security. Greater clarity and conviction among the Member States is needed on what a vigorous and responsive CSDP can and should look like in a more connected, contested and complex global environment.

Humanitarian assistance is also a policy that is yet to adapt to changing global circumstances. While the main objective remains to provide an immediate response in order to save lives and reduce suffering, humanitarian actors are faced with humanitarian crises becoming the "new normal", with ever-increasing needs. New policy action therefore aims at enhancing resilience, disaster risk reduction, and bridging more effectively the transition towards development cooperation.

Enlargement is a policy whose sense of direction is openly contested. Faith in enlargement policy is declining in the EU and candidate countries alike. At the same time, there is no credible alternative to enlargement policy in the Balkans today, and a fair accession process remains the most promising channel to support reforms in Turkey and the Western Balkans alike. The challenge is to make pre-accession policy more credible and restore the belief within the EU and the candidate countries that enlargement can be a win-win for all. Elites and publics in the region risk otherwise turning away from the EU, and looking for inspiration and support elsewhere.

In trade policy, the EU still needs to find effective ways to manage tensions that may arise between trade and non-trade objectives. And within non-trade objectives, a distinction needs to be made between the general pursuit of fundamental freedoms and specific human rights issues which are tied to trade as such, including labour and health standards and property rights. Furthermore, the balance between multilateral, regional and bilateral trade agreements is changing. While in some cases—notably Asia—bilateralism can pave the way to inter-regionalism, in other cases, there may be trade-offs warranting more careful reflection.

The need to manage tensions prevails also in cyber and counterterrorism policies, which are evolving against the backdrop of the need to balance freedom and security. The EU is committed to achieving both. The discussion on how to go about implementing human rights, international law and the rule of law in the cyber domain warrants increased attention, however, not least through diplomatic action. Likewise, in counterterrorism, the debate on security versus freedom remains work in progress.

Second comes *flexibility*. As the largest global donor equipped with a wide range of geographically and thematically tailored instruments, the EU and its Member States are collectively a world leader in development cooperation and humanitarian assistance. The EU is also the only actor committed to reaching a 0.7% ODA/GNI target despite difficult budgetary and economic circumstances. But insufficient flexibility hampers effectiveness, notably in the light of global shocks. In development cooperation, insufficient versatility, emphasis on results reporting and a lack of responsiveness to local circumstances all reduce the EU's impact. The effectiveness of EU development cooperation also hinges on greater awareness of, and responsiveness to, new state and non-state donors, whose funds may or may not have strings attached.

Likewise, in counterterrorism, despite growing attention, implementation is hampered by heavy procedural requirements, insufficient expertise and mainstreaming in programming, and, at times, difficulty in working in concert with the Member States and finding suitable implementing partners.

Third, *leverage*. In trade and development policy, the EU potentially wields significant power. In trade policy, the EU represents the largest trading partner for 80 countries and the second largest for a further 40. Yet, the EU's declining economic dynamism, the high demands it makes of its trading partners, and what it is willing to offer may be hampering its leverage. Proof is the difficulty the EU is facing to conclude negotiations on investment or free-trade agreements with several major partners. In addition, new challenges are emerging as the EU seeks to move beyond the elimination of tariffs to cover non-tariff barriers as well—as in the case of TTIP. Negotiations over non-tariff barriers often entail regulatory convergence, which require a thorough understanding of the needs, interests and procedures of sectorial regulators and social actors. Likewise, sanction policy hinges on the EU's economic strength and the extent to which the EU can embed its efforts within a wider multilateral framework, as well as on the ability of target countries to circumvent EU measures.

Leverage is a challenge also within the European Neighbourhood Policy. The ENP helped cultivate a domestic constituency for reform in several neighbours. The Deep and Comprehensive Free-Trade Agreement negotiations and the Visa Liberalisation Action Plans with Ukraine, Moldova and Georgia spurred progressive reforms in many areas. The ENP facilitated the emergence of a pro-democratic civil society, even in contexts of great repression. At the same time, particularly when it comes to neighbours that have little interest in moving closer to the EU, the ENP has revealed its limits. More tailor-made and reflexive approaches towards each neighbour are required. The ENP alone is also ill-equipped to deal with the hard state-building challenges across the region.

Fourth is *coordination*, both across the institutions and with the Member States. In EU diplomacy, a number of initiatives by various groups of Member States have accompanied and complemented CFSP efforts. Rather than focusing only on speaking with one voice, there is a need for a multitude of voices speaking in unison. Variable actions and formats can only strengthen the EU's global role and reflect the complexity of our times. Provided the EU remains united and well coordinated, varied diplomatic constellations can also give greater visibility to our common priorities and make our collective efforts more effective.

Ranging from development to defence, effectiveness requires coordination among the Member States. In defence, Member States' budgets have been cut in an uncoordinated manner. More recent investment plans by some Member States are equally uncoordinated. In development policy, Joint Programming is a promising step forward in this regard. In development policy—as in the field of non-proliferation, arms control, disarmament and export control—effective implementation requires overcoming the fragmentation of financial instruments both across Commission services and between the EU and its Member States.

In the cyber domain, the EU is ratcheting up its efforts, with several funding instruments focusing in part on building capacity in the areas of cybercrime and cyber security. However, uncertainty still remains over Member State buy-in for a common EU approach. There is also insufficient coordination among EU institutions and inadequate efforts being made to effectively bridge the public–private divide.

Coordination and cohesion challenges are perhaps most pressing in the energy domain. Unlike in climate policy, where the EU stands united and plays a global role, the EU is too often unable to speak and act with one voice when it comes to its external energy policy. Internal fragmentation makes the Union a target of divide-and-rule efforts by some supplier countries. Insufficient EU representation in international energy bodies, insufficient Member State coordination of their external energy policies and insufficient Member State buy-in to the EU's external energy partnerships hamper efforts to achieve energy security. The effects can be seen in the difficulties encountered in building an integrated energy market in the neighbourhood and in completing the Southern Gas Corridor.

Finally, come *capability* challenges. In the field of migration, mobility partnerships and visa facilitation with our partners remain underexploited. In the light of mounting migration challenges, the Commission's Agenda on Migration aims at strengthening Europe's capabilities by assigning additional resources to its Agencies and by integrating the external and internal dimensions of migration management, as well as by tackling the root causes of the phenomenon in the long term. Rising to the migration challenge and doing so in full respect of human rights and international law is a vital interest at the very core of our values.

In security and defence, CSDP has been developed from scratch since 2000. The policy is now equipped with planning capabilities, structures, procedures and a wealth of operational experience built up in some thirty missions to date. CSDP's *modus operandi* of partnering with international and regional organisations—notably the UN, the AU and NATO—is ever more relevant in an age of complexity. However, launching CSDP operations is getting no easier over time. CSDP still faces difficulties in force generation, and access to early and common financing, enablers, intelligence and logistics. This has often limited the scope, size, strategic depth and escalation management ability of missions. The

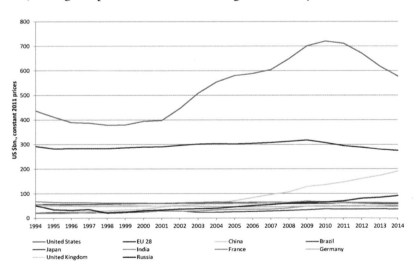

Fig. A.5   Defence expenditure 1994–2014. *Source* SIPRI

Battlegroups, although on stand-by, have never been deployed. The Lisbon Treaty's permanent structured cooperation and Article 44 TEU (on the implementation of a task by a group of Member States) have never been activated. More broadly in the defence field, budgets have been slashed in an uneven manner, with R&T taking the greatest hit. The EU's capability development process remains mostly bottom-up, relying on voluntary contributions by the Member States. The EU is not a military alliance. The Union cannot afford, however, to ignore the "D" in its CSDP (Fig. A.5).

A Joined-Up Approach to Europe's External Action

The Common Security and Defence Policy pioneered the "comprehensive approach to external conflicts and crises". The comprehensive approach is even more relevant today than a decade ago. With conflicts proliferating and escalating, a proactive rather than reactive EU policy must combine early warning, conflict prevention, crisis management and peacebuilding in a coherent whole. This, in turn, is to be connected to long-term state-building and development efforts. How to transition from CSDP to other EU instruments or external partners needs to inform long-term planning. Likewise, in counterterrorism, effectiveness depends on coherence and coordination between internal and external EU security policies, including cyber policies, as well as on the establishment of a more comprehensive information-sharing system between the Member States.

A joined-up approach is needed today not only in external conflicts and crises, however, but also in virtually every aspect of the EU's presence in the world. This puts a premium on the various actors and instruments of EU external action working in synergy. For this to happen, diplomacy is key. Far from being a luxury, diplomacy can be a powerful multiplier of influence, thus realising the full potential of the EU's external action. Today, on top of the diplomatic instruments and regional strategies within the remit of CSFP, specific EU policy areas and departments (environment, trade, development, energy, justice and home affairs, transport, culture, science and research) are all developing their own strands of diplomacy. While welcome, this enhances the need for coordination among the Member States, between EU actors and within the CFSP framework proper.

Closest to home, developing a joined-up external action means establishing closer links between enlargement, neighbourhood, migration, energy, CT and security and defence policies. Concerted external action is necessary to make our immediate neighbours more democratic, prosperous and well governed, as well as more resilient and secure.

In both the neighbourhood and the wider world, when trade policy is used as a foreign policy means, it requires a coherent pursuit of trade and non-trade objectives, which in turn calls for deeper cooperation between different stakeholders in the negotiation and implementation of trade agreements. When trade agreements are pursued to achieve economic goals, successful negotiations often hinge on trade being part of a wider relationship, which includes access to research funding, visa liberalisation, development cooperation and much more. At the same time, introducing energy and climate components in trade and investment agreements can promote the transfer of low-carbon technologies and exchange best practices in terms of governance and regulatory regimes. In the same vein, while sanctions are one of the most powerful tools at the EU's disposal, their effectiveness depends on them being integrated into a joined-up foreign policy involving political dialogue and complementary efforts, which is coordinated with other major players.

As development cooperation widens its horizons post-2015 to address global challenges and develop new forms of cooperation with emerging economies, it becomes all the more necessary to devise a joined-up approach. Such an approach needs to build partnerships beyond the EU and across the public–private divide, and account for the interlinkages between development, on the one hand, and governance, security, trade, migration, energy, climate and cyber on the other. A step forward in this respect is the policy coherence for development. Further efforts in this direction can help ensure that the Union can bring its full weight to bear on driving an ambitious and deliverable post-2015 agenda.

Synergy between migration, trade and development policies is insufficient, as are the linkages between internal and external policies in this regard. When it comes to transit countries, the EU insufficiently factors-in the ties between migration control, labour mobility and trade to enhance incentives for cooperation on border management and readmission. Development cooperation could make an important contribution when addressing migration challenges and countering radicalisation in North and sub-Saharan Africa and in the Middle East. For the migrants' countries of origin, the effective implementation of regional migration strategies hinges on better coordination with development policy and greater insight from diplomatic resources and local partners, including civil society. A joined-up approach to migration prevents the emergence of policy silos. But this also requires the end of geographical silos. Instruments to fight smuggling and trafficking conceived for Syria ought to be relevant for the Horn of Africa, the Balkans and Ukraine, too.

Perhaps clearest of all, a more horizontal, joined-up approach to cyber policies is almost tautological if the EU is to rise to the challenge of a more connected world. Given the use of computer networks and Internet-based applications in all areas of human activity, cyber policies cannot be dealt with in splendid isolation. The effective implementation of external cyber policies depends on cooperation across the public–private divide and on effective coordination between policy areas. While several policy areas deal with the evolution of the cyber domain as such, broader cyber policy needs to be mainstreamed into policies dealing with energy, transport, defence, security, CT, health, the economy and more.

Conclusion

At the time of the 2003 European Security Strategy, the EU was still enjoying its best moment in recent history. The Union was completing the "big bang" enlargement, had just approved an ambitious draft Constitutional Treaty and was launching a no less ambitious neighbourhood policy, as well as the first CSDP missions. The widespread perception at the time was that the EU was equipping itself to safeguard the interests of its citizens globally and promote its values in the world.

Since then, the world—and our perception of it—has become more dangerous, divided and disorienting. The EU has suffered from a major financial and economic crisis, with profound sociopolitical ramifications that still reverberate across the Union. The security environment has deteriorated significantly, with both the eastern and southern neighbourhoods unravelling. The growing number of fragile states, coupled with the spread of new technologies, the pressures of climate change and the scarcity of natural resources could unleash new conflicts in Africa and Asia. Multiple narratives and currencies of power question traditional multilateralism without providing new answers to global governance. At the same time, a more complex and connected world holds the potential of being more prosperous, more equitable and more representative. It can generate forms of growth that are environmentally sustainable and respectful of rights and freedoms.

The world is more connected but also more contested; more integrated but also more fragmented: it is much more complex. Alone, the Member States would struggle to meet these challenges. As a microcosm of complexity and connectivity and the most successful experiment of conflict transformation on a continental scale, the EU has experience in dealing with challenges and opportunities that now present themselves on a global scale. How can we rebuild confidence in the EU's ability to keep its citizens safe and to promote their interests globally? How can we revive the values and political foundations of Europe through foreign policy?

The EU can rely on a broad set of instruments to confront the challenges and seize the opportunities ahead. Much has been achieved, but challenges revolving around policy direction, flexibility, coordination, leverage and capability must be met if the EU is to punch its weight in global affairs. In a degraded security environment, a commitment to strengthening CSDP is crucial, as is the need to develop synergies between internal and external security policies. More broadly, a joined-up approach should guide EU policy not only in conflicts and crises, but also across all fields of EU external action. Vertical and horizontal silos hamper the EU's potential global role. And in a world of mounting challenges and opportunities, it is a luxury we cannot afford.

In a more connected, contested and complex world, we need a clear sense of direction. We need to agree on our priorities, our goals and the means required to achieve them. We need to become more realistic and adaptive, more innovative and more proactive. We must refine the art of orchestration of the polyphony of voices around the table and the panoply of instruments at our disposal.

We need a common, comprehensive and consistent EU Global Strategy.

ANNEX B:

Shared Vision, Common Action: A Stronger Europe. A Global Strategy for the European Union's Foreign and Security Policy

We need a stronger Europe. This is what our citizens deserve; this is what the wider world expects.

We live in times of existential crisis, within and beyond the European Union. Our Union is under threat. Our European project, which has brought unprecedented peace, prosperity and democracy, is being questioned. To the east, the European security order has been violated, while terrorism and violence plague North Africa and the Middle East, as well as Europe itself. Economic growth is yet to outpace demography in parts of Africa, security tensions in Asia are mounting, while climate change causes further disruption. Yet these are also times of extraordinary opportunity. Global growth, mobility, and technological progress—alongside our deepening partnerships—enable us to thrive, and allow ever more people to escape poverty and live longer and freer lives. We will navigate this difficult, more connected, contested and complex world guided by our shared interests, principles and priorities. Grounded in the values enshrined in the Treaties and building on our many strengths and historic achievements, we will stand united in building a stronger Union playing its collective role in the world.

A Global Strategy to Promote our Citizens' Interests

Our interests and values go hand in hand. We have an interest in promoting our values in the world. At the same time, our fundamental values are embedded in our interests. Peace and security, prosperity,

© The Editor(s) (if applicable) and The Author(s) 2017
N. Tocci, *Framing the EU Global Strategy*, Palgrave Studies
in European Union Politics, DOI 10.1007/978-3-319-55586-7

democracy and a rules-based global order are the vital interests underpinning our external action.

Peace and Security

The European Union will promote peace and guarantee the security of its citizens and territory. This means that Europeans, working with partners, must have the necessary capabilities to defend themselves and live up to their commitments to mutual assistance and solidarity enshrined in the Treaties. Internal and external securities are ever more intertwined: our security at home entails a parallel interest in peace in our neighbouring and surrounding regions. It implies a broader interest in preventing conflict, promoting human security, addressing the root causes of instability and working towards a safer world.

Prosperity

The EU will advance the prosperity of its people. This means promoting growth, jobs, equality, and a safe and healthy environment. While a prosperous Union is the basis for a stronger Europe in the world, prosperity must be shared and requires fulfilling the Sustainable Development Goals (SDGs) worldwide, including in Europe. Furthermore, with most world growth expected to take place outside the EU in near future, trade and investment will increasingly underpin our prosperity: a prosperous Union hinges on a strong internal market and an open international economic system. We have an interest in fair and open markets, in shaping global economic and environmental rules, and in sustainable access to the global commons through open sea, land, air and space routes. In view of the digital revolution, our prosperity also depends on the free flow of information and global value chains facilitated by a free and secure Internet.

Democracy

The EU will foster the resilience of its democracies and live up to the values that have inspired its creation and development. These include respect for and promotion of human rights, fundamental freedoms and the rule of law. They encompass justice, solidarity, equality, non-discrimination, pluralism and respect for diversity. Living up consistently to our values internally will determine our external credibility and influence. To safeguard the quality of our democracies, we will respect domestic, European and international law across all spheres, from migration and asylum to energy, counterterrorism and trade. Remaining true to our values is a matter of law as well as of ethics and identity.

A Rules-Based Global Order

The EU will promote a rules-based global order with multilateralism as its key principle and the United Nations at its core. As a Union of medium- to small-sized countries, we have a shared European interest in facing the world together. Through our combined weight, we can promote agreed rules to contain power politics and contribute to a peaceful, fair and prosperous world. The Iranian nuclear agreement is a clear illustration of this fact. A multilateral order grounded in international law, including the principles of the UN Charter and the Universal Declaration of Human Rights, is the only guarantee for peace and security at home and abroad. A rules-based global order unlocks the full potential of a prosperous Union with open economies and deep global connections and embeds democratic values within the international system.

THE PRINCIPLES GUIDING OUR EXTERNAL ACTION

We will be guided by clear principles. These stem as much from a realistic assessment of the strategic environment as from an idealistic aspiration to advance a better world. In charting the way between the Scylla of isolationism and the Charybdis of rash interventionism, the EU will engage the world manifesting responsibility towards others and sensitivity to contingency. Principled pragmatism will guide our external action in the years ahead.

Unity

In a more complex world of global power shifts and power diffusion, the EU must stand united. Forging unity as Europeans—across institutions, states and peoples—has never been so vital nor so urgent. Never has our unity been so challenged. Together we will be able to achieve more than the Member States acting alone or in an uncoordinated manner. There is no clash between national and European interests. Our shared interests can only be served by standing and acting together. Only the combined weight of a true union has the potential to deliver security, prosperity and democracy to its citizens and make a positive difference in the world. The interests of our citizens are best served through unity of purpose between the Member States and across the institutions, and unity in action by implementing together coherent policies.

Engagement

In a more connected world, the EU will reach out and engage with others. In the light of global value chains, galloping technological advances and growing migration, the EU will participate fully in the global marketplace and co-shape the rules that govern it. The Union cannot pull up a drawbridge to ward off external threats. Retreat from the world only deprives us of the opportunities that a connected world presents. Environmental degradation and resource scarcity know no borders, neither do transnational crime and terrorism. The external cannot be separated from the internal. In fact, internal policies often deal only with the consequences of external dynamics. We will manage interdependence, with all the opportunities, challenges and fears it brings about, by engaging in and with the wider world.

Responsibility

In a more contested world, the EU will be guided by a strong sense of responsibility. There is no magic wand to solve crises: there are no neat recipes to impose solutions elsewhere. However, responsible engagement can bring about positive change. We will therefore act promptly to prevent violent conflict, be able and ready to respond responsibly yet decisively to crises, facilitate locally owned agreements and commit long term. We will take responsibility foremost in Europe and its surrounding regions, while pursuing targeted engagement further afield. We will act globally to address the root causes of conflict and poverty, and to champion the indivisibility and universality of human rights.

Partnership

The EU will be a responsible global stakeholder, but responsibility must be shared and requires investing in our partnerships. Co-responsibility will be our guiding principle in advancing a rules-based global order. In pursuing our goals, we will reach out to states, regional bodies and international organisations. We will work with core partners, like-minded countries and regional groupings. We will partner selectively with players whose cooperation is necessary to deliver global public goods and address common challenges. We will deepen our partnerships with civil society and the private sector as key actors in a networked world. We will do so not only through dialogue and support, but also through more innovative forms of engagement.

THE PRIORITIES OF OUR EXTERNAL ACTION

To promote our shared interests, adhering to clear principles, we will pursue five broad priorities

The Security of Our Union

The EU Global Strategy starts at home. Over the decades, our Union has enabled citizens to enjoy unprecedented security, democracy and prosperity. We will build on these achievements in the years ahead. Yet today terrorism, hybrid threats, climate change, economic volatility and energy insecurity endanger our people and territory. The politics of fear challenges European values and the European way of life. To preserve and develop what we achieved so far, a step change is essential. To guarantee our security, promote our prosperity and safeguard our democracies, we will strengthen ourselves on security and defence in full compliance with human rights and the rule of law. We must translate our commitments to mutual assistance and solidarity into action and contribute more to Europe's collective security through five lines of action.

Security and Defence
As Europeans, we must take greater responsibility for our security. We must be ready and able to deter, respond to, and protect ourselves against external threats. While NATO exists to defend its members—most of which are European—from external attack, Europeans must be better equipped, trained and organised to contribute decisively to such collective efforts, as well as to act autonomously if and when necessary. An appropriate level of ambition and strategic autonomy is important for

Europe's ability to foster peace and safeguard security within and beyond its borders.

Europeans must be able to protect Europe, respond to external crises and assist in developing our partners' security and defence capacities, carrying out these tasks in cooperation with others. Alongside external crisis management and capacity building, the EU should also be able to assist in protecting its Members upon their request, and its institutions. This means living up to our commitments to mutual assistance and solidarity and includes addressing challenges with both an internal and external dimension, such as terrorism, hybrid threats, cyber and energy security, organised crime and external border management. For instance, Common Security and Defence Policy (CSDP) missions and operations can work alongside the European Border and Coast Guard and EU specialised agencies to enhance border protection and maritime security in order to save more lives, fight cross-border crime and disrupt smuggling networks.

When it comes to collective defence, NATO remains the primary framework for most Member States. At the same time, EU–NATO relations shall not prejudice the security and defence policy of those Members which are not in NATO. The EU will therefore deepen cooperation with the North Atlantic Alliance in complementarity, synergy and full respect for the institutional framework, inclusiveness and decision-making autonomy of the two. In this context, the EU needs to be strengthened as a security community: European security and defence efforts should enable the EU to act autonomously while also contributing to and undertaking actions in cooperation with NATO. A more credible European defence is essential also for the sake of a healthy transatlantic partnership with the USA.

Member States need the technological and industrial means to acquire and sustain those capabilities which underpin their ability to act autonomously. While defence policy and spending remain national prerogatives, no Member State can afford to do this individually: this requires a concerted and cooperative effort. Deeper defence cooperation engenders interoperability, effectiveness, efficiency and trust: it increases the output of defence spending. Developing and maintaining defence capabilities requires both investments and optimising the use of national resources through deeper cooperation.

The EU will assist the Member States and step up its contribution to Europe's security and defence in line with the Treaties. Gradual synchronisation and mutual adaptation of national defence planning cycles and capability development practices can enhance strategic convergence between the Member States. Union funds to support defence research and technologies and multinational cooperation, and full use of the European Defence Agency's potential are essential prerequisites for European security and defence efforts underpinned by a strong European defence industry.

Counter-Terrorism
Major terrorist attacks have been carried out on European soil and beyond. Increased investment in and solidarity on counterterrorism are key. We will therefore encourage greater information sharing and intelligence cooperation between the Member States and the EU agencies. This entails shared alerts on violent extremism, terrorist networks and foreign terrorist fighters, as well as monitoring and removing unlawful content from the media. Alongside, the EU will support the swift recovery of Members States in the event of attacks through enhanced efforts on security of supply, the protection of critical infrastructure and strengthening the voluntary framework for cyber crisis management. We will deepen work on education, communication, culture, youth and sport to counter violent extremism. We will work on counter-radicalisation by broadening our partnerships with civil society, social actors, the private sector and the victims of terrorism, as well as through inter-religious and inter-cultural dialogue. Most crucially of all, the EU will live up to its values internally and externally: this is the strongest antidote we have against violent extremism. We will also further develop human rights-compliant anti-terrorism cooperation with North Africa, the Middle East, the Western Balkans and Turkey, among others, and work with partners around the world to share best practices and develop joint programmes on countering violent extremism and radicalisation.

Cyber Security
The EU will increase its focus on cyber security, equipping the EU and assisting Member States in protecting themselves against cyber threats while maintaining an open, free and safe cyberspace. This entails strengthening the technological capabilities aimed at mitigating threats and the resilience of critical infrastructure, networks and services, and reducing cybercrime. It means fostering innovative information and communication technology (ICT) systems which guarantee

the availability and integrity of data, while ensuring security within the European digital space through appropriate policies on the location of data storage and the certification of digital products and services. It requires weaving cyber issues across all policy areas, reinforcing the cyber elements in CSDP missions and operations, and further developing platforms for cooperation. The EU will support political, operational and technical cyber cooperation between the Member States, notably on analysis and consequence management, and foster shared assessments between the EU structures and the relevant institutions in Member States. It will enhance its cyber security cooperation with core partners such as the USA and NATO. The EU's response will also be embedded in strong public–private partnerships. Cooperation and information-sharing between the Member States, institutions, the private sector and civil society can foster a common cyber security culture and raise preparedness for possible cyber disruptions and attacks.

Energy Security
The Energy Union represents an integrated effort to work on the internal and external dimensions of European energy security. In line with the goals of the Energy Union, the EU will seek to diversify its energy sources, routes and suppliers, particularly in the gas domain, as well as to promote the highest nuclear safety standards in third countries. Through our energy diplomacy, we will strengthen relations worldwide with reliable energy-producing and transit countries and support the establishment of infrastructure to allow diversified sources to reach European markets. However, binding infrastructure agreements with third countries can have a differentiated impact on the security of supply within the Union or hinder the functioning of the internal energy market. Therefore, such agreements must be transparent, and any new infrastructure must be fully compliant with applicable EU law, including the Third Energy Package. Internally, the EU will work on a fully functioning internal energy market, focus on sustainable energy and energy efficiency and develop coherently reverse flow, interconnection, and liquefied natural gas (LNG) storage infrastructure.

Strategic Communications
The EU will enhance its strategic communications, investing in and joining-up public diplomacy across different fields, in order to connect EU foreign policy with citizens and better communicate it to our

partners. We will improve the consistency and speed of messaging on our principles and actions. We will also offer rapid, factual rebuttals of disinformation. We will continue fostering an open and inquiring media environment within and beyond the EU, also working with local players and through social media.

State and Societal Resilience to our East and South

It is in the interests of our citizens to invest in the resilience of states and societies to the east stretching into Central Asia, and south down to Central Africa. Fragility beyond our borders threatens all our vital interests. By contrast, resilience—the ability of states and societies to reform, thus withstanding and recovering from internal and external crises—benefits us and countries in our surrounding regions, sowing the seeds for sustainable growth and vibrant societies. Together with its partners, the EU will therefore promote resilience in its surrounding regions. A resilient state is a secure state, and security is key for prosperity and democracy. But the reverse holds true as well. To ensure sustainable security, it is not only state institutions that we will support. Echoing the Sustainable Development Goals, resilience is a broader concept, encompassing all individuals and the whole of society. A resilient society featuring democracy, trust in institutions and sustainable development lies at the heart of a resilient state.

Enlargement Policy
Any European state which respects and promotes the values enshrined in our Treaties may apply to become a Member of the Union. A credible enlargement policy grounded on strict and fair conditionality is an irreplaceable tool to enhance resilience within the countries concerned, ensuring that modernisation and democratisation proceed in line with the accession criteria. A credible enlargement policy represents a strategic investment in Europe's security and prosperity and has already contributed greatly to peace in formerly war-torn areas.

Within the scope of the current enlargement policy, the challenges of migration, energy security, terrorism and organised crime are shared between the EU, the Western Balkans and Turkey. They can only be addressed together. Yet the resilience of these countries cannot be taken for granted. The EU enjoys a unique influence in all these countries. The strategic challenge for the EU is therefore that of promoting political reform, rule of law, economic convergence and good neighbourly relations in the Western Balkans and Turkey, while coherently pursuing cooperation across different sectors.

EU policy towards the candidate countries will continue to be based on a clear, strict and fair accession process. It will focus on fundamental requirements for membership first and feature greater scrutiny of reforms, clearer reform requirements, and feedback from the European Commission and Member States, as well as local civil societies. At the same time, EU support for and cooperation with these countries must deliver concrete benefits today and must be communicated well. This means cooperating on counterterrorism, security sector reform, migration, infrastructure, energy and climate, deepening people-to-people contacts and retailoring some of the EU's assistance with the aim of visibly improving citizens' well-being.

Our Neighbours
State and societal resilience is our strategic priority in the neighbourhood. Many people within the scope of the European Neighbourhood Policy (ENP) both to the east and to the south wish to build closer relations with the Union. Our enduring power of attraction can spur transformation and is not aimed against any country. Within this group are currently countries such as Tunisia or Georgia, whose success as prosperous, peaceful and stable democracies would reverberate across their respective regions. The ENP has recommitted to Eastern Partnership and southern Mediterranean countries wishing to develop stronger relations with us. We will support these countries in implementing association agreements, including Deep and Comprehensive Free Trade Areas (DCFTAs). We will also think creatively about deepening tailor-made partnerships further. Possibilities include the creation of an economic area with countries implementing DCFTAs, the extension of Trans-European Networks and the Energy Community, as well as building physical and digital connections. Societal links will also be strengthened through enhanced mobility, cultural and educational exchanges, research cooperation and civil society platforms. Full participation in EU programmes and agencies will be pursued alongside strategic dialogue with a view to paving the way for these countries' further involvement in CSDP.

Resilience is a strategic priority across the EU's east and south both in countries that want stronger ties with the EU and in those—within and beyond the ENP—that have no wish to do so. The EU will support different paths to resilience to its east and south, focusing on the most acute dimensions of fragility and targeting those where we can make a meaningful difference.

Resilience in our Surrounding Regions

The EU will pursue a multifaceted approach to resilience in its surrounding regions. While repressive states are inherently fragile in the long term, there are many ways to build inclusive, prosperous and secure societies. We will therefore pursue tailor-made policies to support inclusive and accountable governance, critical for the fight against terrorism, corruption and organised crime, and for the protection of human rights. Repression suffocates outlets for discontent and marginalises communities. The EU will therefore promote human rights through dialogue and support, including in the most difficult cases. Through long-term engagement, we will persistently seek to advance human rights protection. We will pursue locally owned rights-based approaches to the reform of the justice, security and defence sectors, and support fragile states in building capacities, including cyber. We will work through development, diplomacy and CSDP, ensuring that our security sector reform efforts enable and enhance our partners' capacities to deliver security within the rule of law. We will cooperate with other international players, coordinating our work on capacity building with the UN and NATO in particular.

States are resilient when societies feel they are becoming better off and have hope in the future. Echoing the Sustainable Development Goals, the EU will adopt a joined-up approach to its humanitarian, development, migration, trade, investment, infrastructure, education, health and research policies, as well as improve horizontal coherence between the EU and its Member States. We will fight poverty and inequality, widen access to public services and social security, and champion decent work opportunities, notably for women and youth. We will foster an enabling environment for new economic endeavours, employment and the inclusion of marginalised groups. Development funds should catalyse strategic investments through public–private partnerships, driving sustainable growth, job creation and skills and technological transfers. We will use our trade agreements to underpin sustainable development, human rights protection and rules-based governance.

Societal resilience will be strengthened by deepening relations with civil society, notably in its efforts to hold governments accountable. We will reach out more to cultural organisations, religious communities, social partners and human rights defenders, and speak out against the shrinking space for civil society including through violations of the freedoms of speech and association. Positive change can only be home-grown and may take years to materialise. Our commitment to civil society will therefore be long term. We will nurture societal resilience also by deepening work on education, culture and youth to foster pluralism, coexistence and respect.

Finally, the EU will seek to enhance energy and environmental resilience. Energy transition is one of the major challenges in our surrounding regions, but must be properly managed to avoid fuelling social tensions. Climate change and environmental degradation exacerbate potential conflict, in the light of their impact on desertification, land degradation and water and food scarcity. Mirroring security sector reform efforts, energy and environmental sector reform policies can assist partner countries along a path of energy transition and climate action. Through such efforts, we will encourage energy liberalisation, the development of renewables, better regulation and technological transfers, alongside climate change mitigation and adaptation. We will also support governments to devise sustainable responses to food production and the use of water and energy through development, diplomacy and scientific cooperation.

A More Effective Migration Policy
A special focus in our work on resilience will be on origin and transit countries of migrants and refugees. We will significantly step up our humanitarian efforts in these countries, focusing on education, women and children. Together with countries of origin and transit, we will develop common and tailor-made approaches to migration featuring development, diplomacy, mobility, legal migration, border management, readmission and return. Through development, trust funds, preventive diplomacy and mediation, we will work with countries of origin to address and prevent the root causes of displacement, manage migration and fight trans-border crime. We will support transit countries by improving reception and asylum capacities, and by working on migrants' education, vocational training and livelihood opportunities. We must stem irregular flows by making returns more effective as well as by ensuring regular channels for human mobility. This means enhancing and implementing existing legal and circular channels for migration. It also means working on a more effective common European asylum system which upholds the right to seek asylum by ensuring the safe, regulated

and legal arrival of refugees seeking international protection in the EU. At the same time, we will work with our international partners to ensure shared global responsibilities and solidarity. We will establish more effective partnerships on migration management with UN agencies, emerging players, regional organisations, civil society and local communities.

An Integrated Approach to Conflicts and Crises

We increasingly observe fragile states breaking down in violent conflict. These crises, and the unspeakable violence and human suffering to which they give rise, threaten our shared vital interests. The EU will engage in a practical and principled way in peacebuilding, concentrating our efforts in surrounding regions to the east and south, while considering engagement further afield on a case-by-case basis. The EU will foster human security through an integrated approach.

All of these conflicts feature multiple dimensions—from security to gender, from governance to the economy. Implementing a *multidimensional* approach through the use of all available policies and instruments aimed at conflict prevention, management and resolution is essential. But the scope of the "comprehensive approach" will be expanded further. There are no quick fixes to any of these conflicts. Experience in Somalia, Mali, Afghanistan and elsewhere highlights their protracted nature. The EU will therefore pursue a *multiphased* approach, acting at all stages of the conflict cycle. We will invest in prevention, resolution and stabilisation, and avoid premature disengagement when a new crisis erupts elsewhere. The EU will therefore engage further in the resolution of protracted conflicts in the Eastern Partnership countries. None of these conflicts plays out at a single level of governance. Conflicts such as those in Syria and Libya often erupt locally, but the national, regional and global overlay they acquire is what makes them so complex. The EU will therefore pursue a *multilevel* approach to conflicts acting at the local, national, regional and global levels. Finally, none of these conflicts can be solved by the EU alone. We will pursue a *multilateral* approach engaging all those players present in a conflict and necessary for its resolution. We will partner more systematically on the ground with regional and international organisations, bilateral donors and civil society. Greater cooperation will also be sought at the regional and international levels. Sustainable peace can only be achieved through comprehensive agreements rooted in broad, deep and durable regional and international partnerships.

Pre-emptive Peace

It has long been known that preventing conflicts is more efficient and effective than engaging with crises after they break out. Once a conflict does erupt, it typically becomes ever more intractable over time. The EU enjoys a good record on pre-emptive peacebuilding and diplomacy. We will therefore redouble our efforts on prevention, monitoring root causes such as human rights violations, inequality resource stress and climate change—which is a threat multiplier that catalyses water and food scarcity, pandemics and displacement.

Early warning is of little use unless it is followed by early action. This implies regular reporting and proposals to the Council, engaging in preventive diplomacy and mediation by mobilising EU Delegations and Special Representatives, and deepening partnerships with civil society. We must develop a political culture of acting sooner in response to the risk of violent conflict.

Security and Stabilisation

The EU will engage more systematically on the security dimension of these conflicts. In full compliance with international law, European security and defence must become better equipped to build peace, guarantee security and protect human lives, notably civilians. The EU must be able to respond rapidly, responsibly and decisively to crises, especially to help fight terrorism. It must be able to provide security when peace agreements are reached and transition governments established or in the making. When they are not, the EU should be ready to support and help consolidating local ceasefires, paving the way for capacity building. At the same time, through a coherent use of internal and external policies, the EU must counter the spillover of insecurity that may stem from such conflicts, ranging from trafficking and smuggling to terrorism.

When the prospect of stabilisation arises, the EU must enable legitimate institutions to rapidly deliver basic services and security to local populations, reducing the risk of relapse into violence and allowing displaced persons to return. We will therefore seek to bridge gaps in our response between an end of violence and long-term recovery, and develop the dual—security and development—nature of our engagement.

Conflict Settlement
Each conflict country will need to rebuild its own social contract between the state and its citizens. The Union will support such efforts, fostering inclusive governance at all levels. When the "centre" is broken, acting only top-down has limited impact. An inclusive political settlement requires action at all levels. Through CSDP, development and dedicated financial instruments, we will blend top-down and bottom-up efforts fostering the building blocks of sustainable statehood rooted in local agency. Working at the local level—for instance with local authorities and municipalities—can help basic services be delivered to citizens and allows for deeper engagement with rooted civil society. Working in this direction will also improve our local knowledge, helping us distinguish between those groups we will talk to without supporting, and those we will actively support as champions of human security and reconciliation.

The EU will also foster inclusive governance at all levels through mediation and facilitation. At the same time, we will develop more creative approaches to diplomacy. This also means promoting the role of women in peace efforts—from implementing the UNSC Resolution on Women, Peace and Security to improving the EU's internal gender balance. It entails having more systematic recourse to cultural, inter-faith, scientific and economic diplomacy in conflict settings.

Political Economy of Peace
The EU will foster the space in which the legitimate economy can take root and consolidate. In the midst of violent conflict, this means ensuring humanitarian aid access to allow basic goods and services to be provided. It also means working to break the political economy of war and to create possibilities for legitimate sustenance to exist. This calls for greater synergies between humanitarian and development assistance, channelling our support to provide health, education, protection, basic goods and legitimate employment. When the prospects for stabilisation arise, trade and development—working in synergy—can underpin long-term peacebuilding.

Restrictive measures, coupled with diplomacy, are key tools to bring about peaceful change. They can play a pivotal role in deterrence, conflict prevention and resolution. Smart sanctions, in compliance with international and EU law, will be carefully calibrated and monitored to support the legitimate economy and avoid harming local societies. To fight the criminal war economy, the EU must also modernise its policy on export control for dual-use goods, and fight the illegal trafficking of cultural goods and natural resources.

Cooperative Regional Orders

In a world caught between global pressures and local pushback, regional dynamics come to the fore. As complex webs of power, interaction and identity, regions represent critical spaces of governance in a de-centred world. Voluntary forms of regional governance offer states and people the opportunity to better manage security concerns, reap the economic gains of globalisation, express more fully cultures and identities and project influence in world affairs. This is a fundamental rationale for the EU's own peace and development in the twenty-first century. This is why we will promote and support cooperative regional orders worldwide, including in the most divided areas. Regional orders do not take a single form. Where possible and when in line with our interests, the EU will support regional organisations. We will not strive to export our model, but rather seek reciprocal inspiration from different regional experiences. Cooperative regional orders, however, are not created only by organisations. They comprise a mix of bilateral, sub-regional, regional and inter-regional relations. They also feature the role of global players interlinked with regionally owned cooperative efforts. Taken together, these can address transnational conflicts, challenges and opportunities. In different world regions, the EU will be driven by specific goals. Across all regions, we will invest in cooperative relationships to spur shared global responsibilities.

The European Security Order

The sovereignty, independence and territorial integrity of states, the inviolability of borders and the peaceful settlement of disputes are key elements of the European security order. These principles apply to all states, both within and beyond the EU's borders.

However, peace and stability in Europe are no longer a given. Russia's violation of international law and the destabilisation of Ukraine, on top of protracted conflicts in the wider Black Sea region, have challenged the European security order at its core. The EU will stand united in upholding international law, democracy, human rights, cooperation and each country's right to choose its future freely.

Managing the relationship with Russia represents a key strategic challenge. A consistent and united approach must remain the cornerstone of EU policy towards Russia. Substantial changes in relations between the EU and Russia are premised upon full respect for international law and the principles underpinning the European security order, including the Helsinki Final Act and the Paris Charter. We will not recognise Russia's illegal annexation of Crimea nor accept the destabilisation of eastern Ukraine. We will strengthen the EU, enhance the resilience of our eastern neighbours and uphold their right to determine freely their approach towards the EU. At the same time, the EU and Russia are interdependent. We will therefore engage Russia to discuss disagreements and cooperate if and when our interests overlap. In addition to those foreign policy issues on which we currently cooperate, selective engagement could take place over matters of European interest too, including climate, the Arctic, maritime security, education, research and cross-border cooperation. Engagement should also include deeper societal ties through facilitated travel for students, civil society and business.

Spanning the region, the EU will foster cooperation with the Council of Europe and the Organisation for Security and Cooperation in Europe. The OSCE, as a Europe-wide organisation stretching into Central Asia with a transatlantic link, lies at the heart of the European security order. The EU will strengthen its contribution within and its cooperation with the OSCE as a pillar of European security.

A Peaceful and Prosperous Mediterranean, Middle East and Africa
The Mediterranean, Middle East and parts of sub-Saharan Africa are in turmoil, the outcome of which will likely only become clear decades from now. Solving conflicts and promoting development and human rights in the south is essential to addressing the threat of terrorism, the challenges of demography, migration and climate change, and to seizing the opportunity of shared prosperity. The EU will intensify its support for and cooperation with regional and sub-regional organisations in Africa and the Middle East, as well as functional cooperative formats in the region. However, regional organisations do not address all relevant dynamics, and some reflect existing cleavages. We will therefore also act flexibly to help bridge divides and support regional players in delivering concrete results. This will be achieved by mobilising our bilateral and multilateral policies and frameworks as well as by partnering with civil societies in the region.

The EU will follow five lines of action. First, in the Maghreb and the Middle East, the EU will support functional multilateral cooperation. We will back practical cooperation, including through the Union for the Mediterranean, on issues such as border security, trafficking, counterterrorism, non-proliferation, water and food security, energy and climate, infrastructure and disaster management. We will foster dialogue and negotiation over regional conflicts such as those in Syria and Libya. On the Palestinian–Israeli conflict, the EU will work closely with the Quartet, the Arab League and all key stakeholders to preserve the prospect of a viable two-state solution based on 1967 lines with equivalent land swaps and to recreate the conditions for meaningful negotiations. The EU will also promote full compliance with European and international law in deepening cooperation with Israel and the Palestinian Authority.

Second, the EU will deepen sectoral cooperation with Turkey, while striving to anchor Turkish democracy in line with its accession criteria, including the normalisation of relations with Cyprus. The EU will therefore pursue the accession process—sticking to strict and fair accession conditionality—while coherently engaging in dialogue on counterterrorism, regional security and refugees. We will also work on a modernised customs union and visa liberalisation, and cooperate further with Turkey in the fields of education, energy and transport.

Third, the EU will pursue balanced engagement in the Gulf. It will continue to cooperate with the Gulf Cooperation Council (GCC) and individual Gulf countries. Building on the Iran nuclear deal and its implementation, it will also gradually engage Iran on areas such as trade, research, environment, energy, anti-trafficking, migration and societal exchanges. It will deepen dialogue with Iran and GCC countries on regional conflicts, human rights and counterterrorism, seeking to prevent contagion of existing crises and foster the space for cooperation and diplomacy.

Fourth, in the light of the growing interconnections between North and sub-Saharan Africa, as well as between the Horn of Africa and the Middle East, the EU will support cooperation across these sub-regions. This includes fostering triangular relationships across the Red Sea between Europe, the Horn and the Gulf to face shared security challenges and economic opportunities. It means systematically addressing cross-border dynamics in North and West Africa, the Sahel and Lake

Chad regions through closer links with the African Union, the Economic Community of Western African States (ECOWAS) and the G5 Sahel.

Finally, we will invest in African peace and development as an investment in our own security and prosperity. We will intensify cooperation with and support for the African Union, as well as ECOWAS, the Inter-Governmental Authority on Development in eastern Africa, and the East African Community, among others. We must enhance our efforts to stimulate growth and jobs in Africa. The Economic Partnership Agreements can spur African integration and mobility and encourage Africa's full and equitable participation in global value chains. A quantum leap in European investment in Africa is also needed to support sustainable development. We will build stronger links between our trade, development and security policies in Africa and blend development efforts with work on migration, health, education, energy and climate, science and technology, notably to improve food security. We will continue to support peace and security efforts in Africa and assist African organisations' work on conflict prevention, counterterrorism and organised crime, migration and border management. We will do so through diplomacy, CSDP and development, as well as trust funds to back up regional strategies.

A Closer Atlantic

The EU will invest further in strong bonds across the Atlantic, both north and south. A solid transatlantic partnership through NATO and with the USA and Canada helps us strengthen resilience, address conflicts and contribute to effective global governance. NATO, for its members, has been the bedrock of Euro–Atlantic security for almost 70 years. It remains the strongest and most effective military alliance in the world. The EU will deepen its partnership with NATO through coordinated defence capability development, parallel and synchronised exercises, and mutually reinforcing actions to build the capacities of our partners, counter hybrid and cyber threats, and promote maritime security.

With the USA, the EU will strive for a Transatlantic Trade and Investment Partnership (TTIP). Like the Comprehensive Economic and Trade Agreement (CETA) with Canada, TTIP demonstrates the transatlantic commitment to shared values and signals our willingness to pursue an ambitious rules-based trade agenda. On the broader security agenda, the USA will continue to be our core partner. The EU will deepen cooperation with the USA and Canada on crisis management, counter-terrorism, cyber, migration and energy and climate action.

In the wider Atlantic space, the Union will expand cooperation and build stronger partnerships with Latin America and the Caribbean, grounded on shared values and interests. It will develop multilateral ties with the Community of Latin American and Caribbean States (CELAC) and with different regional groupings according to their competitive advantage. We will step up political dialogue and cooperation on migration, maritime security and ocean life protection, climate change and energy, disarmament, non-proliferation and arms control, and countering organised crime and terrorism. We will pursue a free-trade agreement with Mercosur, build on the Political Dialogue and Cooperation Agreement with Cuba and invest in deeper socio-economic connections with Latin American and Caribbean countries through visa facilitation, student exchanges, twinning, research cooperation and technical projects. We will also actively support the negotiation and implementation of peace agreements in the region, as we are doing in Colombia.

A Connected Asia

There is a direct connection between European prosperity and Asian security. In the light of the economic weight that Asia represents for the EU—and vice versa—peace and stability in Asia are a prerequisite for our prosperity. We will deepen economic diplomacy and scale up our security role in Asia.

The EU will engage China based on respect for rule of law, both domestically and internationally. We will pursue a coherent approach to China's connectivity drives westwards by maximising the potential of the EU–China Connectivity Platform, and the ASEM and EU–ASEAN frameworks. The EU will also deepen trade and investment with China, seeking a level playing field, appropriate intellectual property rights protection, greater cooperation on high-end technology, and dialogue on economic reform, human rights and climate action. In parallel, the EU will deepen its economic diplomacy in the region, working towards ambitious free-trade agreements with strategic partners such as Japan and India, as well as ASEAN member states, with the goal of an eventual EU–ASEAN agreement.

We will also develop a more politically rounded approach to Asia, seeking to make greater practical contributions to Asian security. We will expand our partnerships, including on security, with Japan, the Republic of Korea, Indonesia and others. We will continue to support state-building and reconciliation processes in Afghanistan together with our regional and international partners. We will promote non-proliferation in the Korean peninsula. In East and Southeast Asia, we will uphold freedom of navigation, stand firm on the respect for international law, including the Law of the Sea and its arbitration procedures and encourage the peaceful settlement of maritime disputes. We will help build maritime capacities and support an ASEAN-led regional security architecture. In Central and South Asia, we will deepen cooperation on counterterrorism, anti-trafficking and migration, as well as enhance transport, trade and energy connectivity. Across the Indo Pacific and East Asian regions, the EU will promote human rights and support democratic transitions such as in Myanmar/Burma.

A Cooperative Arctic
With three Member States and two European Economic Area members being Arctic states, the EU has a strategic interest in the Arctic remaining a low-tension area, with ongoing cooperation ensured by the Arctic Council, a well-functioning legal framework, and solid political and security cooperation. The EU will contribute to this through enhanced work on climate action and environmental research, sustainable development, telecommunications and search andrescue, as well as concrete cooperation with Arctic states, institutions, indigenous peoples and local communities.

Global Governance for the Twenty-First Century

Without global norms and the means to enforce them, peace and security, prosperity and democracy—our vital interests—are at risk. Guided by the values on which it is founded, the EU is committed to a global order based on international law, including the principles of the UN Charter, which ensure peace, human rights, sustainable development and lasting access to the global commons. This commitment translates into an aspiration to transform rather than simply preserve the existing system. The EU will strive for a strong UN as the bedrock of the multilateral rules-based order and develop globally coordinated responses with international and regional organisations, states and non-state actors.

Reforming: A commitment to global governance must translate in the determination to reform the UN, including the Security Council, and the International Financial Institutions (IFIs). Resisting change risks triggering the erosion of such institutions and the emergence of alternative groupings to the detriment of all EU Member States. The EU will stand up for the principles of accountability, representativeness, responsibility, effectiveness and transparency. The practical meaning of such principles will be fleshed out case-by-case. We will continue to call upon members of the UN Security Council not to vote against credible draft resolutions on timely and decisive action to prevent or end mass atrocities. Across multilateral fora—and in particular the UN, the IFIs and the international justice organisations—the EU will strengthen its voice and acquire greater visibility and cohesion. We will work towards an increasingly unified representation of the euro area in the International Monetary Fund.

Investing: Believing in the UN means investing in it, notably in its peacekeeping, mediation, peacebuilding and humanitarian functions. The EU and its Member States, as already the first contributor to UN humanitarian agencies, will invest even further in their work. CSDP could assist further and complement UN peacekeeping through bridging, stabilisation or other operations. The EU will also enhance synergy with UN peacebuilding efforts, through greater coordination in the planning, evolution and withdrawal of CSDP capacity-building missions in fragile settings.

Implementing: The EU will lead by example by implementing its commitments on sustainable development and climate change. It will increase climate financing, drive climate mainstreaming in multilateral fora, raise the ambition for review foreseen in the Paris agreement and work for clean energy cost reductions. The SDGs will inform the post-Cotonou partnership and drive reform in development policy, including the EU Consensus on Development. Moreover, implementing the SDGs will require change across all internal and external policies, galvanising public–private partnerships, and leveraging the experience of the European Investment Bank (EIB) in providing technical assistance and building capacities in developing and middle-income countries.

Deepening: As the world's largest economy, the EU is a prime mover in global trade and investment, areas in which rules can be deepened further. Our prosperity hinges on an open and rules-based economic system with a true level playing field, which our economic diplomacy will further promote. We will pursue comprehensive free-trade agreements with the USA, Japan, Mercosur, India, ASEAN and others as building blocks of global free trade. Ambitious agreements built on mutual benefits such as TTIP and CETA can promote international regulatory standards, consumer protection, as well as labour, environmental, health and safety norms. New generation trade agreements which include services, the digital economy, energy and raw materials can reduce legal fragmentation and barriers, and regulate access to natural resources. The EU will ensure that all its trade agreements are pursued in a manner that supports returning the World Trade Organisation (WTO) to the centre of global negotiations. Connected to the EU's interest in an open and fair economic system is the need for global maritime growth and security, ensuring open and protected ocean and sea routes critical for trade and access to natural resources. The EU will contribute to global maritime security, building on its experience in the Indian Ocean and the Mediterranean, and exploring possibilities in the Gulf of Guinea, the South China Sea and the Straits of Malacca. As a global maritime security provider, the EU will seek to further universalise and implement the UN Convention on the Law of the Sea, including its dispute settlement mechanisms. We will also promote the conservation and sustainable use of marine resources and biological diversity and the growth of the blue economy by working to fill legal gaps and enhancing ocean knowledge and awareness.

Widening: We will seek to widen the reach of international norms, regimes and institutions. The proliferation of weapons of mass destruction and their delivery systems remains a growing threat to Europe and the wider world. The EU will strongly support the expanding membership, universalisation, full implementation and enforcement of multilateral disarmament, non-proliferation and arms control treaties and regimes. We will use every means at our disposal to assist in resolving proliferation crises, as we successfully did on the Iranian nuclear programme. The EU will actively participate in export control regimes, strengthen common rules governing Member States' export policies of military—including dual use—equipment and technologies, and support export control authorities in third countries and technical bodies that sustain arms control regimes. The EU will also promote the responsibility to protect, international humanitarian law, international human rights law and international criminal law. We will support the UN Human Rights Council and encourage the widest acceptance of the jurisdiction of the International Criminal Court and the International Court of Justice.

Developing: At the frontiers of global affairs, rules must be further developed to ensure security and sustainable access to the global commons. The EU will be a forward-looking cyber player, protecting our critical assets and values in the digital world, notably by promoting a free and secure global Internet. We will engage in cyber diplomacy and capacity building with our partners and seek agreements on responsible state behaviour in cyberspace based on existing international law. We will support multilateral digital governance and a global cooperation framework on cyber security, respecting the free flow of information. In space, we will promote the autonomy and security of our space-based services and work on principles for responsible space behaviour, which could lead to the adoption of an international voluntary code of conduct. On energy, we will encourage multilateral mechanisms aimed at ensuring sustainable energy patterns both by developing our own sustainable policies and by deepening dialogue with major energy consumers and producers. On health, we will work for more effective prevention, detection and responses to global pandemics. Global rules are also necessary in fields such as biotechnology, artificial intelligence, robotics and remotely piloted systems, to avoid the related security risks and reap their economic benefits. On all such issues, the EU will promote exchanges with relevant multilateral fora to help spearhead the development of rules and build partnerships at the frontiers of global affairs.

Partnering: The EU will lead by example on global governance. But it cannot deliver alone. It will act as an agenda-shaper, a connector, coordinator and facilitator within a networked web of players. It will partner not only with the states and organisations, but also with the private sector and civil society. On the vast majority of global governance issues, we will work with the UN as the framework of the multilateral system and a core partner for the Union, with other core partners such as the USA, with regional organisations, and with like-minded and strategic partners in Asia, Africa and the Americas. The EU will also invest in pivotal non-state actors, particularly within civil society. In spite of increasing repression, global civil society is growing and fostering new types of activism. The EU will sharpen the means to protect and empower civic actors, notably human rights defenders, sustaining a vibrant civil society worldwide.

The format to deliver effective global governance may vary from case to case. On cyber, global governance hinges on a progressive alliance between states, international organisations, industry, civil society and technical experts. On maritime multilateralism, the EU will work with the UN and its specialised agencies, NATO, our strategic partners and ASEAN. On humanitarian action, sustainable development and climate change, the EU will partner with the UN and the G20, as well as new donors, civil society and the private sector. On counterterrorism, we will deepen dialogue with the UN, while building broad partnerships with states, regional organisations, civil society and the private sector on issues such as countering violent extremism and terrorist financing.

From Vision to Action

We will pursue our priorities by mobilising our unparalleled networks, our economic weight and all the tools at our disposal in a coherent and coordinated way. To fulfil our goals, however, we must collectively invest in a credible, responsive and joined-up Union.

A Credible Union

To engage responsibly with the world, credibility is essential. The EU's credibility hinges on our unity, on our many achievements, our enduring power of attraction, the effectiveness and consistency of our policies, and adherence to our values. A stronger Union requires investing in all dimensions of foreign policy, from research and climate to infrastructure and mobility, from trade and sanctions to diplomacy and development.

In this fragile world, soft power is not enough: we must enhance our credibility in security and defence. To respond to external crises, build our partners' capacities and protect Europe, Member States must channel a sufficient level of expenditure to defence, make the most efficient use of resources and meet the collective commitment of 20% of defence budget spending devoted to the procurement of equipment and research and technology. Capabilities should be developed with maximum interoperability and commonality and be made available where possible in support of EU, NATO, UN and other multinational efforts. While a sectoral strategy, to be agreed by the Council, should further specify the civil–military level of ambition, tasks, requirements and capability priorities stemming from this Strategy, some such areas can already be highlighted in line with commitments made by the European Council.

First, European security hinges on better and shared assessments of internal and external threats and challenges. Europeans must improve the monitoring and control of flows which have security implications. This requires investing in Intelligence, Surveillance and Reconnaissance, including Remotely Piloted Aircraft Systems, satellite communications and autonomous access to space and permanent earth observation. As regards counterterrorism, Member States must implement legislation concerning explosives, firearms and passenger name records (PNRs), as well as invest in detection capabilities and the cross-border tracing of weapons. Second, Europeans must invest in digital capabilities to secure data, networks and critical infrastructure within the European digital space. We must develop capabilities in trusted digital services and products and in cyber technologies to enhance our resilience. We will encourage greater investments and skills across the Member States through cooperative research and development, training, exercises and procurement programmes. Third, regarding high-end military capabilities, the Member States need all major equipment to respond to external crises and keep Europe safe. This means having full-spectrum land, air, space and maritime capabilities, including strategic enablers.

To acquire and maintain many of these capabilities, Member States will need to move towards defence cooperation as the norm. Member States remain sovereign in their defence decisions: nevertheless, nationally-oriented defence programmes are insufficient to address capability shortfalls. We remain far from achieving our collective benchmarks, including 35% of total equipment spending in collaborative procurement. The voluntary approach to defence cooperation must translate into real commitment. An annual coordinated review process at EU level to discuss Member States' military spending plans could instil greater coherence in defence planning and capability development. This should take place in full coherence with NATO's defence planning process. The European Defence Agency (EDA) has a key role to play by strengthening the Capability Development Plan, acting as an interface between the Member States and the Commission, and assisting Member States to develop the capabilities stemming from the political goals set out in this Strategy.

Defence cooperation between the Member States will be systematically encouraged. Regular assessments of EDA benchmarks can create positive peer pressure among the Member States. Crucially, EU funding for defence research and technology, reflected first in the mid-term review of the Multiannual Financial Framework, and then in a fully fledged programme in the next budget cycle, will prove instrumental in developing the defence capabilities Europe needs.

A sustainable, innovative and competitive European defence industry is essential for Europe's strategic autonomy and for a credible CSDP. It can also stimulate growth and jobs. A solid European defence, technological and industrial base needs a fair, functioning and transparent internal market, security of supply and a structured dialogue with defence relevant industries. Furthermore, ensuring participation of small and medium-sized enterprises (SMEs) in the defence sector can improve innovation and investment in the military technologies of tomorrow.

A Responsive Union

We live in a world of predictable unpredictability. We will therefore equip ourselves to respond more rapidly and flexibly to the unknown lying ahead. A more responsive Union requires change. We need it in diplomacy, CSDP and development, as well as investment in the knowledge base underpinning our external action.

First, our diplomatic action must be fully grounded in the Lisbon Treaty. EU foreign policy is not a solo performance: it is an orchestra which plays from the same score. Our diversity is a tremendous asset provided we stand united and work in a coordinated way. Cooperation between the Member States can strengthen our engagement in the world. A Member State or a group of Member States who are willing and able to contribute may be invited by the High Representative (HR), under the responsibility of the Council, to implement agreed positions of the Council. The HR shall keep the Council fully informed and shall ensure consistency with agreed EU policies.

Second, CSDP must become more rapid and effective. Europeans must be ready to rapidly respond to crises in full compliance with the UN Charter. This requires Member States to enhance the deployability and interoperability of their forces through training and exercises. We must develop the capacity for rapid response also by tackling the procedural, financial and political obstacles which prevent the deployment of the Battlegroups, hamper force generation and reduce the effectiveness of CSDP military operations. At the same time, we must further develop our civilian missions—a trademark of CSDP—by encouraging force generation, speeding up deployment and providing adequate training based on EU-wide curricula. A responsive CSDP also requires streamlining our institutional structure. We must strengthen operational planning and conduct structures and build closer connections between civilian and military structures and missions, bearing in mind that these may be deployed in the same theatre. Enhanced cooperation between the Member States should be explored in this domain. If successful and repeated over time, this might lead to a more structured form of cooperation, making full use of the Lisbon Treaty's potential.

Third, development policy will become more flexible and aligned with our strategic priorities. We reaffirm our collective commitment to achieve the 0.7% ODA/GNI target in line with DAC principles. Development funds must be stable, but lengthy programming cycles limit the timely use of EU support, and can reduce our visibility and impact. The availability of limited sums for activities on the ground, notably for conflict prevention and civil society support, should be made more flexible. Across the Commission, flexibility will be built into our financial instruments, allowing for the use of uncommitted funds in any given year to be carried on to subsequent years to respond to crises. This will also help fill the gaps between financial instruments and budgetary headings. In parallel, the time has come to consider reducing the number of instruments to enhance our coherence and flexibility, while raising the overall amount dedicated to development.

Responsive external action must be underpinned by a strong knowledge base. Targeted approaches to resilience, conflict prevention and resolution require deeper situational awareness. The EU will invest in the EEAS and coordinate better across the institutions and the Member States. Putting our diverse national cultures at the service of our shared interests is a challenge, but the pool of talent available to us is unrivalled. To make the most of this, we will invest in people, particularly those on the ground. This means equipping our delegations with the necessary expertise, including on sectoral issues and in local languages, valuing experience in and of a region, beefing up the political sections of delegations and encouraging operational staff to use their expertise more politically. It means strengthening the participation of women in foreign policy making. It means investing in the EU Conflict Early

Warning System and making all our external engagement conflict- and rights-sensitive. We will also pursue greater information sharing and joint reporting, analysis and response planning between Member State embassies, EU Delegations, Commission services, EU Special Representatives and CSDP missions. We will encourage cross-fertilisation between us and regional and international organisations, civil society, academia, think tanks and the private sector. We will do so both in traditional ways— through dialogue, cooperation and support—and through innovative formats such as exchanges, embedded personnel and joint facilities, harnessing knowledge and creativity in our system.

A Joined-Up Union

Finally, our external action will become more joined-up. Over the years, important steps have been taken to this effect: these include institutional innovations, such as the Lisbon Treaty's creation of the double-hatted High Representative and Vice-President of the European Commission (HRVP) and the European External Action Service (EEAS). A strong EEAS working together with other EU institutions lies at the heart of a coherent EU role in the world. Efforts at coherence also include policy innovations such as the "comprehensive approach to conflicts and crises" and joint programming in development, which must be further enhanced. New fields of our joined-up external action include energy diplomacy, cultural diplomacy and economic diplomacy.

A more prosperous Union requires economic priorities to be set in relations with all countries and regions, and integrated into the external dimensions of all internal policies. A more prosperous Union calls for greater coordination between the EU and the Member States, the EIB and the private sector. The Sustainable Development Goals also represent an opportunity to catalyse such coherence. Implementing them will generate coherence between the internal and external dimensions of our policies and across financial instruments. It allows us to develop new ways to blend grants, loans and private–public partnerships. The SDGs also encourage us to expand and apply the principle of policy coherence for development to other policy areas and encourage joint analysis and engagement across Commission services, institutions and Member States.

We must become more joined-up across internal and external policies. The migration phenomenon, for example, requires a balanced and human rights-compliant policy mix addressing the management of the flows and the structural causes. This means overcoming the fragmentation of external policies relevant to migration. In particular, we will develop stronger links between humanitarian and development efforts through joint risk analysis, and multiannual programming and financing. We will also make different external policies and instruments migration-sensitive—from diplomacy and CSDP to development and climate—and ensure their coherence with internal ones regarding border management, homeland security, asylum, employment, culture and education.

In security terms, terrorism, hybrid threats and organised crime know no borders. This calls for tighter institutional links between our external action and the internal area of freedom, security and justice. Closer ties will be fostered through joint Council meetings and joint task forces between the EEAS and the Commission. Defence policy also needs to be better linked to policies covering the internal market, industry and space. Member State efforts should also be more joined-up: cooperation between our law enforcement, judicial and intelligence services must be strengthened. We must use the full potential of Europol and Eurojust and provide greater support for the EU Intelligence Centre. We must feed and coordinate intelligence extracted from European databases and put ICT—including big data analysis—at the service of deeper situational awareness. Our citizens need better protection also in third countries through joint contingency plans and crisis response exercises between the Member States.

We must become more joined-up in our security and development policies. CSDP capacity building missions must be coordinated with security sector and rule of law work by the Commission. Capacity Building for Security and Development can play a key role in empowering and enabling our partners to prevent and respond to crises and will need to be supported financially by the EU. Our peace policy must also ensure a smoother transition from short-term crisis management to long-term peacebuilding to avoid gaps along the conflict cycle. Long-term work on pre-emptive peace, resilience and human rights must be tied to crisis response through humanitarian aid, CSDP, sanctions and diplomacy.

Finally, we will systematically mainstream human rights and gender issues across policy sectors and institutions, as well as foster closer coordination regarding digital matters. Greater awareness and expertise on such issues is needed within the EEAS and the Commission. Better coordination between institutions would also add consistency and spread best practices, helping us build a stronger Union and a more resilient, peaceful and sustainable world.

The Way Ahead

This Strategy is underpinned by the vision of, and ambition for, a stronger Union, willing and able to make a positive difference to its citizens and in the world. We must now swiftly translate this into action. First, we will revise existing sectoral strategies, as well as devise and implement new thematic or geographic strategies in line with the political priorities of this Strategy. Such work must begin with clear procedures and time frames agreed promptly by all relevant players. Second, the EU Global Strategy itself will require periodic reviewing in consultation with the Council, the Commission and the European Parliament. On a yearly basis, we will reflect on the state of play of the Strategy, pointing out where further implementation must be sought. Finally, a new process of strategic reflection will be launched whenever the EU and its Member States deem it necessary to enable the Union to navigate effectively our times.

Our citizens deserve a true union, which promotes our shared interests by engaging responsibly and in partnership with others.

BIBLIOGRAPHY

Kupchan, Charles A., (ed.) 1998. *Atlantic Security: Contending Visions*. New York: Council on Foreign Relations Press.

Peterson, John, Riccardo Alcaro, and Nathalie Tocci. 2016. Multipolarity, multilateralism and leadership: The retreat of the west? In *The west and the global power shift. Transatlantic relations and global governance*, ed. John Peterson, Riccardo Alcaro and Ettore Greco, 43–73. New York, Palgrave Macmillan.

© The Editor(s) (if applicable) and The Author(s) 2017   163
N. Tocci, *Framing the EU Global Strategy*, Palgrave Studies
in European Union Politics, DOI 10.1007/978-3-319-55586-7

INDEX

© The Editor(s) (if applicable) and The Author(s) 2017

N. Tocci, *Framing the EU Global Strategy*, Palgrave Studies in European Union Politics, DOI 10.1007/978-3-319-55586-7

28107308R00103

Printed in Great Britain
by Amazon